A View from the Trenches

A View from the Trenches

Ups and Downs
of Today's Parish Priest

Monsignor Dennis Murphy

Foreword by Bishop Richard Grecco

Paulist Press
New York/Mahwah, NJ

Cover design by Blair Turner
Layout by Audrey Wells

First published in English in Canada by Novalis.
Sales authorized in the United States of America as per agreement.

Cataloging-in-Publication Data:

BX1913.M87 2009   262'.14   C2009-903928-1

ISBN 978-0-8091-4666-6

Published in the United States of America in 2009 by

Paulist Press

997 Macarthur Boulevard
Mahwah, New Jersey, 07430
United States of America

www.paulistpress.com

Printed and bound in Canada

$\mathcal{A}$cknowledgments

To Joseph Sinasac, the English-language Publishing Director of Novalis, my appreciation once again for his constant encouragement and insights. This small book would not have happened without his support.

Part of my good fortune in life is to have enjoyed the friendship of many dedicated priests, both in my own diocese and elsewhere. I hope their wisdom, devotion and great good humour are reflected in these pages. The lay people and religious who have been close to me over the years have worked hard at keeping me honest, if not humble. To all these friends I say, "Thank you."

I would be particularly remiss if I did not acknowledge the assistance of two wonderful people, friends of many years, in developing and recasting the thoughts contained in these pages. There are few ideas that I have had about the priesthood that I have not discussed at some point with Father Everett MacNeil and Sister Veronica O'Reilly, CSJ. Both of them kindly consented to read this manuscript and the original retreat talks upon which it is based. Their comments and insights were always judicious, even when we did not agree! My thanks to both of them. As always, any errors remain mine.

Contents

$\mathscr{F}$oreword

When I was a young, newly ordained and somewhat naïve priest, I unwittingly infuriated my pastor by blaming Bing Crosby for the disservice done to priests in movies such as *The Bells of St. Mary's* and *Going My Way*. I then tried to calm my pastor by saying that these movies were wonderful, wholesome entertainment, but hardly worthy of the image of a priest in a post–Vatican II Church. This explanation did little to console him; in fact, I suspect he thought I was patronizing him. Obviously, he and I had very different notions about the ideal priest.

For better or for worse, the film and television industries have influenced us all with ideas and images of the Church and its priests. In the first chapter of *A View from the Trenches*, Monsignor Dennis Murphy alludes to actor Karl Malden, who plays a Catholic priest and confessor to President Jed Bartlet in the hit television series *The West Wing*. (Coincidentally, Malden also played a priest as labour activist in the 1950s film *On the Waterfront*.) In the 1980s, the British TV series *Bless Me, Father*, set in an English Catholic parish of the 1950s, starred Arthur Lowe as the curmudgeonly pastor, Fr. Duddleswell – a laugh a minute, but truly an exercise in nostalgia. In the '70s and into the '80s, Father Mulcahy entertained us as the Catholic chaplain in the popular TV series M*A*S*H*. Despite his big heart and good intentions, Fr. Mulcahy lacked depth and had little influence on his flock.

Clint Eastwood starred and directed in the 2008 film *Gran Torino*, in which an inexperienced, ineffectual young priest slowly matures as he ministers with perseverance and courage to an irreligious, bigoted parishioner. Eventually, the parishioner reconciles with God through the Sacrament of Reconciliation and the priest spiritually and socially grows in appreciation of the height and depth of the human condition.

The media have certainly had their way with the image of the Catholic priest. As art forms, movies and TV shows help us see reality from a perspective different from our own. But what is our own view of the priesthood? How do priests see themselves and their place in the parish today? Unlike artists and even social scientists, who look at the priesthood from an outside, rather distant perspective, priests and parishioners experience and know the priesthood from daily life within their communities. We claim a spirituality and world view based on what God has revealed to us about our origin, purpose and destiny in his Son, Jesus Christ. Anyone who loves knows the person loved in a way that no artist or social scientist could ever capture. *A View from the Trenches* reveals a self-understanding of the parish priest, a depiction by one who sees God's love in the People of God. This book will be of interest therefore not only to priests, but to the faithful as well.

Monsignor Murphy does not offer theoretical analysis or Church dogmatics. Instead, he presents the role of the parish priest based on his own experience of Church and the priesthood, posing questions and offering insights that provide a realistic image and understanding of the Catholic parish priest today. It is a source of hope that should be read by anyone seeking greater wisdom about this essential characteristic of the Catholic Church.

Bishop Richard Grecco
Auxiliary Bishop of Toronto

$\mathscr{I}$ntroduction

Most of the material in the pages that follow originated in a series of conferences I gave a couple of years ago
during the annual priests' retreat in my diocese of Sault
Ste. Marie. My hope is that it will be of interest not only
to Catholic priests, but also to clergy, men and women
religious, and Christians of all denominations who wonder
and worry about the role of those who minister to them
in these new times – times that so often seem marked by
the absence of God, with little place left for the spiritual
side of life and the mystery of human existence. For clergy
and others, this book offers an opportunity to reflect on
certain aspects of ministry in these times and provides
"some time apart."

One of the great paradoxes in the Catholic Church
these days is that while survey results tell us that priests are

still among the most satisfied and happy men in the land, most of the priests I know often feel somewhat battered and beleaguered in the exercise of their ministry. Media coverage of and the stigma attached to priests' sexual misconduct, stories of physical, emotional and sexual abuse in Canada's Native residential schools, and tales of financial malfeasance in parish administration cast a shadow over the lives of all the ordained, even though the great majority are innocent of any wrongdoing. Some priests feel that their collective integrity has been undermined by a few of their brothers. Those ordained a number of years have come a long way down from our formerly lofty position in the Church and society, where we were much admired for virtue and competency that were presumed by most. Today, even the most virtuous, dedicated and accomplished priest often lives under a cloud of suspicion, if not downright mistrust.

Priests who work in parishes are the front-line troops and the most visible of Catholic clergy. They suffer most publicly the reflected shame of the moral failings of a few of their number – failings that have received high-profile attention in the Western world. As well, priests as spiritual leaders find themselves caught in the crosshairs of a new assault by aggressive secularists who ascribe all kinds of evil and superstition to religious belief of every hue and shape. As spokespersons and witnesses of institutional religion, clergy today are cast in an unkind light by those who give short shrift to all established religious groups.

The latter are linked to an unknowing era – a throwback to the darkness arising out of non-scientific thought. Priests are, as well, builders of community at a time when the reality of community is considered no more than a social construct in our highly individualized society. If religious belief is discussed at all, the common mantra heard, the new and acceptable hubris, is: "I don't believe in or participate in any institutionalized religion. I do, however, try to have my own relationship with God!" New spiritualities, however bizarre, are blithely accepted as the only legitimate expression of whatever sense of the transcendent, whatever religious feelings and urges are common to the human experience of almost all people. In this kind of world, where the relationship is totally individual, between God and me, priests are hardly needed.

Priests today may find themselves unwittingly caught in a new manifestation of anticlericalism. Because of the prominent position of priests in society and culture over the centuries, clashes have often taken place between priests and social institutions that would deny, diminish or curtail priests' influence. One thinks here of the anticlericalism of the French Revolution (1789–99), the Russian Revolution (1917), the Mexican civil war (1858–61), and the imprisonment and persecution of priests in China following the victory of the forces of Mao Tse-Tung's forces in the last century.

Over the centuries in most Western societies, the three "estates" or sectors of society (the Lords or temporal rulers, the Clergy or spiritual leaders, and the Commoners) have traditionally been locked in struggles for influence and power. In Canada, at least, the declining number of active or practising Catholics and other Christians in the last half-century has allowed governments, with political impunity, to sideline the religious point of view in numerous instances. Whether there is a cause and effect operating here is a moot question. However, few would deny, for example, that here in Canada in recent years, the influence of religious bodies and their clergy on the development of government policy – social, foreign or monetary – has significantly decreased.

Amidst these societal developments of the last century, the press and, more generically, the media has come to be known as the "fourth estate," playing an ever more influential role in the direction and governance of society. With these various estates flexing their muscles and seeking more influence and power, it is perhaps not surprising that priests often feel that the fourth estate seems to take particular pleasure in highlighting anything that would cast suspicion upon the priesthood. The result – intended or not – is to mitigate the influence of priests on the mores and direction of society.

In the Church itself, it was not many years ago that the priest was a central figure in the faith life of families and individuals who were closely associated with parish life. He rejoiced with the families he served as they brought the newly born to the baptismal font to share in the communal grace life of the Christian community. In the coming of age of confirmation and first communion, in the celebration of marriage and in the sorrow of sickness and death, priests were regarded as virtual members of the families they served. Even those who seldom practised their faith welcomed the priest into their homes as one who symbolized and mediated the mystery and transcendent values of the human journey. Today in the Roman Catholic community, a new distance often exists between the priest and many baptized Catholics. The easy familiarity that once marked the relationship at times seems strained.

The reasons why this situation has changed are legion. The obvious ones, mentioned above, remain true. Added to these, and on a positive note, is the growing realization that the priest belongs in the Catholic community not as one standing apart, but as a brother chosen from among his brothers and sisters to serve them in parish ministry. The ensuing familiarity assures that the wearing of a Roman collar no longer guarantees compliant agreement on everything that issues forth from the priest's mouth. The relationship between people and priest is better for this development. Less positively, however, and at a deeper level, priests find themselves in a new world where the politically correct position of many social institutions demands an attitude of standing at arm's length as far as religion is concerned. The sacred not only has been differentiated from the secular, but has been relegated by many to the trash bin of historical oddities. Not science, but the scientism of positivism, dismisses the world of mystery and transcendence. Many would sideline the gospel imperative from public life and discussion. In this new world, the words of priests as symbols and spokespersons for the sacred are accepted grudgingly, if at all, even by Catholics within the Church. The priest, who used to occupy a position of some respect and importance, now finds himself unimportant in the eyes of many.

At a time in Western society where many confess belief but practically live lives of half belief, misbelief or disbelief; at a time when the default position of many is a practical if not theoretical unbelief; at a time when, in response to our deeply felt need for transcendence, movies and popular TV shows feature ghost busters, and benevolent witches, and space beings with preternatural powers – in these times, we have witnessed a bold assault on religious belief. One dimension of this assault has been sharp criticism of the priesthood, which traditionally has been especially entrusted with the maintenance and development of this same religious belief.

Perhaps it is no surprise that as the priesthood comes under attack, fewer men are being ordained. Yet, it is at our peril that the Church fails to confront the reality of the falling number of priests in the West and the effect of this situation upon priests working in parish ministry. Fewer and fewer priests are servicing our parishes; some care for three or more parishes each, or find themselves alone in a parish that in days gone by had two or three assistant priests. The threat of burnout is a reality in the lives of many priests as they try to ration their time and yet respond to pastoral demands and situations even when they may find themselves physically, mentally and even spiritually exhausted. But the question of fewer priests also has another, often unrecognized effect. When there is only so much a priest can accomplish in his work, he often gives what hours he has mainly to the celebration of Eucharist and the other sacraments. In effect, he becomes a "Mass priest." As his ministry becomes restricted to the cultic functions, he may unconsciously begin to define his priesthood only in this way. And yet, as we shall discuss in Chapter 3, important as the sacramental ministry is, it is not necessarily the first and fundamental ministry that the priest shares with his bishop and brother priests. The danger, explored in Chapter 6, is that the shortage of priests can willy-nilly skew the very definition and self-identity of the priest.

A related consequence of the declining number of priests is that they have little time to reach out to those places in the community where Christianity has not penetrated, to search out the "lost sheep." It is difficult to engage the missionary dimension of priesthood when there is simply no time to do so many things. The evangelization of the milieu and concern for those who have strayed from the faith traditionally were important concerns of parish priests. Such activities include public proclamation of the gospel, parish retreats and missions, and visits to schools and homes within the parish. Much of this "shepherding" has fallen on hard times because of a lack of clergy.

In exploring the nature and practice of priestly ministry today, and its relevance in the lives of our contemporaries, it seems worthwhile in these introductory remarks to situate the Catholic priesthood within the broader context of priesthood as it has existed in the history of humankind over the centuries. The notion of priesthood and its meanings have been part of the human experience from time immemorial. Shamans and medicine men, priests and Levites, diviners and prophets have always been part of the human project. The shamans, prophets and diviners have usually been self-appointed or seen to have been deputed directly by their god or gods. Priests, however, have stood apart from the others, as they exercised their functions in society as part of a group or school of religious persons. Priests in most cultures traditionally were designated members of the institution or community. This community or institution educated them in some way so that they might officially mediate between the divine or sacred and the profane or secular realms. They have ever been the leaders or presiders or celebrants of the rituals of a particular religion. They remain the commonly accepted religious and spiritual leaders in their society. Immersed in their culture and society, they are familiar with the stories, the narrative and the codes of their religious and social community. They know the symbols and their meanings, which transcend ordinary experience.

As a result, cultural histories reveal that priests in their communities have been ascribed spiritual powers that they are to exercise in favour of the community they serve. Particularly in situations of distress and complexity, when human powers seem stymied, recourse has been made to the priest. As well, in the significant moments of birth and death, of coming of age and of marriage, the priest is called upon to mediate with the powers of life and beyond life in favour of the people. In the best of circumstances they are the consolers, the celebrant, the interceders, the mediators who help to bridge the realms of the sacred and the profane.

This is the service that priests have rendered to the society or community they serve from humanity's early beginnings. Whether understood as chosen from the community or called by the deity, the priest's role or function was one of service in remembering the story, telling its meaning, celebrating its rituals and mediating its message in all aspects of the life journey of the society's members. History reveals that often enough, this role of service was compromised by a quest for power and influence and the good things the society offered. It remained, nonetheless, a ministry of accompanying people as they confronted the many aspects of the mystery of life itself.

Catholic teaching has always insisted that there is only one priest who mediates between God and human beings: "Only Christ is the true priest, the others being only his ministers" (*Catechism of the Catholic Church*, n. 1545). More particularly, the ordained priest in Catholic belief is the one who makes present the unique priestly ministry of Jesus Christ. Catholic theology considers the ministry of the ordained priest as embracing the functions of teaching, guiding (or ruling) and sanctifying (or making holy). The ordained minister serves the priesthood of the faithful (the laity). This, in short, is the understanding of the Catholic priesthood. We will explore several aspects of this view in the following pages.

The Waters We Swim In: Our Social, Ecclesial and Clerical Environments

In an episode of the acclaimed TV series *The West Wing*, the Catholic president, Jed Bartlet, grapples with whether he should commute the death sentence of a convicted killer. He seeks counsel from the teaching of his Church, from the opinion of a Quaker friend, and from his Jewish communications director. From different belief perspectives, all the advice recommends clemency. Politically, however, there are reasons for allowing the execution to proceed. On the night the execution is to take place, a tormented President Bartlet is seen in the Oval Office saying the rosary. At his request, his pastor from days gone by comes to visit him. In the course of their conversation about the execution, the pastor asks Bartlet if he has prayed about it. The president answers that he has prayed mightily, but has received no guidance from God, and is more than a little "peed off."

With this, the pastor tells the story of the very religious and holy man who hears on the radio that a flood is expected in his area. The man says to himself, "Not to worry, God will take care of me." As the waters rise, a boat from the Emergency Measures Organization comes to his house to rescue him, but he tells them, "I'm not concerned. God will look after me." As the waters rise to the second storey of his house, a helicopter comes to take him to safety. Once again, he tells his would-be rescuers that God will look after him. Finally, however, he drowns. Appearing before St. Peter, the man demands to see God. He berates God for not looking after him, a deeply holy and spiritual man. To this God replies, "I warned you on the radio. I sent someone in a boat. And then I sent a helicopter."

The pastor then says to President Bartlet, "You say that your prayers were not answered. Yet God spoke to you through your Quaker friend, through your Jewish communications director, and through the teaching of your Church."

This story reflects Christian belief that it is in the ordinary course of events, in the surround sound of life, in the experience of our lives that God speaks to us. More specifically, when we set out to grasp again or to listen anew to God, our faith reminds us that the face, the word and the action of God are revealed not only in our sacred writings and tradition, but also in our environment, the waters in which we swim daily. As priests, we find ourselves immersed in various milieus each day. Three deserve special consideration: the contemporary social environment, the ecclesial or Church environment, and the environment of our priestly or clerical culture.

There are at least two good reasons for reflecting on these three environments. First, these social and cultural milieus have a profound effect on our lives. Whether we are conscious of it or not, they influence our thinking, our values and attitudes, and even our beliefs. Second, in these same environments are found the signs of our times. These environments provide indicators for what, where and how God speaks to us in our ministry and in our Church today. In these milieus, we find both the good and the bad, the bitter and the sweet, what is clear and what seems ambiguous. In the light of scripture and tradition, we trust God to speak to us, to continue to reveal his face in these signs.

As someone who has been involved in the world of education for many years, I have always had the basic conviction that the surrounding milieu or culture is the greatest educator of how we think and feel, of how we relate to one another and to God. Yet we can be surprisingly unaware of what the milieu is teaching us and how profoundly we are affected by it. One of the most famous aphorisms of Marshall McLuhan, the great communications guru of the last century, was that the last creature in the world that could tell us anything about water would be the fish. Pursuing this analogy, McLuhan reasoned that like water is for a fish, the environment in which we live and move and have our being is so close to us that we may not recognize its influence in our lives. This gives us a good reason to scrutinize the environments of our times to ensure that we pay sufficient attention to the many factors, feelings, convictions, messages and "knowledges" that surround us and affect the way we live.

The pastoral constitution Gaudium et Spes, which emerged from Vatican II (1962–1965), is best known as The Church in the Modern World. It picked up on the phrase "the signs of the times" that Pope John XXIII often used. The document insists that as a Church, we have a duty to scrutinize in our different environments these "signs of the times" – the everyday signposts of our milieu – and interpret them in the light of the gospel. Through these signs, we hear the word of God addressed to our world and to us in a special way. In Matthew's gospel, we hear the religious leaders of Jesus' time asking him for a special sign. He chastises them for their failure to be aware of what is going on around them, for disregarding signs of God's word and presence everywhere: "When it is evening, you say, 'It will be fair weather, for the sky is red.' And in the morning, 'It will be stormy today, for the sky is red and threatening.' You know how to interpret the appearance of the sky, but you cannot interpret the signs of the times." (Matt. 16:2-3).

In other words, priests as discerning people who are attuned to the prompting of God's Spirit must first recognize what happens in the world: especially in our Western world, in the Church, and in the presbyterate of our particular diocese. These environments provide the backdrop for a priest's major experiences. The great Spanish mystic John of the Cross tells us, "The language of God is the experience God writes into our lives." So we continually ask ourselves this question: What is the experience God is writing into my life, and what does it mean for my journey to God?

To reflect on some of the dominant factors, happenings, attitudes and events currently shaping and affecting our lives represents for us as believers something much more than a sociological exercise. It is an attempt to do two things: first, to be more aware of all that affects and influences and shapes us – what is making us who we are and affecting how we think; and second, to recognize that within these experiences of ours lie signs that speak to us of God within us, of God within our Church, and of God within our world.

No one can presume to speak to the rich and manifold experiences of all priests. It seems worthwhile, however, to suggest some fairly common experiences, some basic touchstones, some thoughts on this world and Church and presbyterate in which we find ourselves today – and to discern the signs within these milieus that speak to us of where we are being called.

Before we explore these three environments, a rather entertaining tale can underline the necessity of taking our various milieus as a starting point.

Jack Kornfield, a renowned American Buddhist teacher, tells a story of being in Calcutta as the construction of a brand new golf course was completed. This development was most unusual for that area and people were very excited about it. However, the first day, when the golfers got out and teed off and the ball started rolling along the fairway, something unexpected happened. Monkeys in the area thought this was a game for them. They scampered after the ball, picked it up and threw it. For weeks, the owners of the golf course tried to outsmart the monkeys. They gave them their own golf balls, saying, "Here's a big pile of balls; go into the trees and play with these." But the monkeys wanted the balls that came off the tee. Eventually, Kornfield said, he noticed a new rule posted in the clubhouse: "Play the ball where the monkey puts it."

For priests, then, the question is this: Where is the monkey putting the ball in our social environment, our ecclesial environment, and our clerical environment? And where are we as priests in the midst of these somewhat disjointed but wonderfully challenging times of ours?

Our Social Environment

Whatever else identifies our contemporary environment, few can deny that it is unremittingly secular. Since the Enlightenment, Western society, with the possible exception of the United States, has passed from being a self-described Christian milieu to one that prides itself on its growing secularity. As Canadian philosopher Charles Taylor points out in the introduction to his book *A Secular Age*, almost everyone would agree that we live in an era of secularity in present-day Western society. For many in our society, Taylor points out, there is a commitment to a kind of humanism that excludes all meaning systems but its own. A fundamentally different universe of human discourse exists between human society of the year 2000 and that of 1500, he says. Belief, the beyond, the transcendent are no longer allowed to easily penetrate daily life. The priest, who is by definition a servant and mediator of religious belief, finds himself ministering in a climate in which religion is intellectually unfashionable, and the lingua franca is one of agnosticism and skepticism. A practical agnosticism is the attitude of many in a pluralistic, multicultural society. This agnosticism or skepticism hardly admits the possibility of objective truth, and it casts a disbelieving eye on anyone who claims to speak a truth that is valid for all people. For the priest and for believers in general, it is easy to be highly critical of this secular environment, often described as modernity or postmodernity, in which we live.

All, however, is not lost. Pope John Paul II did not hesitate to criticize what he saw to be the weaknesses, failings and, indeed, the sins of our Western society. Nonetheless, in his 1992 decree, *Pastores Dabo Vobis* (On the formation of priests), he begins his assessment of our times by pointing out that never before in the history of humankind has there been such a worldwide thirst for justice; that today we are endowed with deepened respect for nature and all of creation; that there exists a new possibility of human solidarity and respect for the human rights of all individuals. He goes on to speak of the search for God and the accompanying phenomenon of a new religiosity that seems more pronounced in Western society than in recent years. Men and women seem starved for some sense of ultimate meaning that goes beyond material success. Other voices have pointed out that with the explosion of the information technology which is the medium of the day, the search for meaning and for the ethical dimension of our lives has become more universal. We are experiencing new levels of global concern for diseases such as HIV/AIDS, a more global search for peace, the rejection of patriarchy, and the rise of what is best in feminism. Our world is more pluralistic, tolerant, diverse, cosmopolitan and international than ever before.

In addition, radical discoveries in the fields of astronomy, space travel, biology and quantum physics lay bare the mysterious interconnectedness of everything in this universe. In her 2007 book, *The Sky Is Not a Ceiling*, Aileen O'Donoghue points out both the beauty and the ambiguity of our world as revealed by contemporary science. Writing about the origins of our planet and the certainty of its ultimate demise, she says,

> Mother Earth, who fostered so many species in salted
> oceans, canopied jungles, and ageless grasslands is as

mortal as the creatures that have passed from her lands and seas into extinction … the mountains, the flowers, the fish, and the cities, will be reduced to the basic elements of which they are made and blown back to the empty reaches between the stars. There is a comforting completeness in knowing that our physical substance, forged in the cores of the stars, shall become again part of the interstellar dust from which new stars will be made.

Asserting that "Deep within the biochemical labyrinth of the human brain is a soul that contemplates and seeks a reason for its own existence," O'Donoghue reminds us that "… we still cannot determine how we came to have the minds capable of conceiving the questions that we ask." In the marvels of the intricacies of cells and atoms, and in the infinite reaches of the universe, there is in our time a new opening to the wonder of who or what lies behind it all. These discoveries seem to bring with them a deepened longing for wholeness, within ourselves, with each other and with our universe. There exists today a promising new care and concern for all the species that inhabit the earth with us, and for our beautiful planet itself. There is much that is life-giving in our secular times.

On the negative side, Pope John Paul and others, such as the Dominican theologian Albert Nolan, in his 2006 book, *Jesus Today: A Spirituality of Radical Freedom*, describe the individualism, materialism and total subjectivity endemic to our secular world. Unannounced and almost unconsciously, materialism is accepted as the valid norm for measuring the successful life. Perhaps the most obvious and glaring example of individualism and subjectivity is that the individual focus of many in Western society on their personal concerns threatens, through profligate consumption, to create a level of global warming that could destroy the very planet that sustains us. Pervasive individualism is equally recognizable in the social injustices that result on a global scale when the selfish temptation of unregulated capitalism is allowed to run wild. In times of economic recession, we don't have to go beyond our own country, province and local parish to see the impoverishing effects this situation can have on so many.

A supposedly neutral secularism often reveals a face that is openly hostile to all religious belief. This almost fundamentalist secularism supports an increasingly value-laden agenda that would deny not only Christians, but all believers, a voice in the public discussion on the policies and directions of government. In his 2007 book, *The Audacity of Hope*, United States President Barack Obama points out that although there can be a reaction to the overreaching of religion in public life, this reaction can "equate tolerance with secularism, and forfeit the moral language that would help infuse our [public] policies with a larger meaning."

It is clear that a new atheism is abroad today, and it has a sharp edge. In recent years, a number of non-fiction books have attacked religious belief: these include *The God Delusion*, by Richard Dawkins; *The End of Faith: Religion, Terror and the Future of Reason*, by Sam Harris; *Atheist Manifesto:*

The Case Against Christianity, Judaism and Islam, by Michel Onfray; and *God Is Not Great: How Religion Poisons Everything*, by Christopher Hitchens. That they have topped the bestseller lists should give us pause.

Some four years after the close of Vatican II, the great French theologian Henri de Lubac, whose theological vision had much influence on the thought of this council, was already fearful of the tendencies in Europe to marginalize the Church. Given the current refusal by the European Parliament to acknowledge in its proposed constitution the obvious influence of Christianity in the history of Europe, de Lubac's words are prophetic. In 1969, he talked about "A bitter and vindictive disposition, sparing nothing, ... being directed against the Church's past and present, indiscriminately attacking it structures of authority, neglecting all the positive things it had accomplished over the centuries, odiously misrepresenting its history ...."

Perhaps more evident is the practical atheism of many, the attacks on the sacredness of the family, a growing disrespect for the life of the unborn and of the elderly, and a kind of scientific reductionism that would suggest that at best we are little more than selfish strings of DNA seeking above all to assure our own survival. The media, particularly in the realm of social commentary, often only grudgingly allow religion a place in discussions about contemporary public issues. Nor is it paranoia to wonder about the anti-religious and particularly anti-Catholic comment that seems to remain acceptable as the last refuge of bigoted and offensive commentators.

In a situation where it seems we are being everywhere beaten about the head, it is well to keep in mind that the Catholic Church – and, in many cases, the Christian Church – is in disfavour in our secular world not only because of the clergy sexual abuse scandals that have so rocked the Church, even though there is no doubt that we have historically and currently manifested our sinful side. The Church is also in disfavour because of its faithfulness to the gospel. It is in disfavour because its social teaching criticizes a society that continues to elect, at many different levels, governments whose priorities are to make the rich richer rather than to address issues such as child poverty, the needs of indigenous peoples and the shameful global disparities of wealth. Catholics and other religious groups are in disfavour because of their opposition to government policies that reduce social assistance to single parents, marginalize the poor and weak, and make economic growth the ultimate goal of society. Catholics are in disfavour today because of continued insistence on these and other life issues, such as abortion and euthanasia. Catholics are in disfavour for refusing to accept that pre-marital and extra-marital sex is value-neutral behaviour – for insisting that such behaviour has negative consequences for human sexuality and the family. Yet despite the avowedly secular agenda of many social and cultural institutions of our time – particularly the news media – it remains true that the Church is still recognized as a voice that speaks and acts in favour of the most marginalized people in our world. For many, the Church's voice, although muted, is still heard, especially when moral and ethical questions of social justice arise.

Our Ecclesial Culture

Perhaps closer to home the question we ask ourselves is this: What does a scan of our Christian culture reveal about the life of the Church, both universally and locally?

Well before the sexual abuse scandals that rocked the Catholic community in recent years, many people were distancing themselves from Church life. We are living in a time of transition. In a relatively short period of time, our old certainties – not only in religion, but in politics, government, education and science – have been shaken, in large part due to the lightning speed of new forms of communication. The result, as all of us have known for years, is that participation in the life of the Church has become peripheral to the daily experience of the majority of Roman Catholics in our towns and cities – and in most of the Western world. Even those Catholics who do participate in the life of the Church attach decreasing credibility to the teaching of the Church, particularly on moral issues. From artificial birth control to in vitro fertilization, from pre-marital to extra-marital sex, from divorce and remarriage to clerical celibacy, from homosexual relationships to social justice, from business ethics to genetic engineering and stem cell research, many Catholics, especially younger

Catholics, stand at an oblique remove from the Church's moral teaching. Part of this shift in attitudes is surely due to the moral relativism of contemporary Western society. But there is more to it than that.

One point that strike us priests most forcefully here is that often we are not listened to, not seen as teachers of the faith, as we were in the past. This is particularly true in the area of ethics and moral teaching, which are no longer the preserve of clergy alone. We do not occupy the moral high ground unquestioned. Those to whom we preach are much more highly educated than at any time in the life of the Church. They must be persuaded of the relevance of the gospel to their lives. And they are convinced that before they will listen to us, we must listen to them. Lest we think we are alone in this, consider how people today question all the experts. Medical doctors regularly have their opinions challenged, engineers are blamed for fallen bridges and collapsed buildings, and economists are commonly chastised as having no role except to make weather forecasters look good!

A number of phenomena in our ecclesial culture seem to call for further comment: 1) the decrease in priestly and religious vocations; 2) a troubling lack of transparency in the Church; 3) hesitation in accepting the evolving role of the laity; 4) religious illiteracy; and 5) the contemporary search for God. Let's look briefly at each one.

The Vocations Crisis

The present situation, where those who have traditionally provided the leadership in our faith community – priests and religious – are fewer and fewer in number, and greyer and greyer in appearance, has a direct impact on the life of the priest Much effort is expended to encourage young people to embrace the vocation of the religious life or priesthood, but the task seems an uphill one. One major obstacle is that few parents encourage their sons and daughters to follow the call to the serving professions, including the priesthood or religious life. One can speculate that parents wish for their children professions or positions with greater social prestige and monetary reward. A recent survey of the priests in the archdiocese of Ottawa reported that "The culture of sixty, fifty or even forty years ago that nurtured vocations to the priesthood and religious life does not exist today." Yet vocations must come out of a culture.

The Lack of Transparency in the Church

In recent years, Catholics have sought to cope with the troubling revelations of sexual abuse by clergy. What has surfaced beyond this shame is the discovery that within our Church exists a climate of secrecy and a lack of transparency. This unhealthy climate extends to decisions affecting the lives of all Catholics, including the processes by which priests and bishops are appointed to a parish or diocese. The respected retired seminary rector Father Donald Cozzens has suggested that such practices threaten to sustain a clerical culture that can too easily be tempted to place clerical concerns and ecclesiastical politics above the pastoral care of God's people. The danger of clericalism is a real one. From the day the priest is ordained, he is considered "set apart," not only in his own mind but in the minds of many, if not most, Catholics. He dresses in a distinctive fashion; has a special title; presides at liturgical functions as the leader garbed in ceremonial robes; is assumed to have the knowledge and competence associated with a particular class; and has access to powers related to his ministry. Belonging to this group is meant to provide a service to the Church membership. Poorly understood and lived, however, it can mask a claim for entitlements and a delusion of superiority that eschews the need for transparency.

The Evolving Role of the Laity

Vatican II emphasized that, by and large, lay people constitute the Church, *are* the Church. Yet many priests seem to remain ambivalent in accepting this key doctrine. On the one hand, we accept the need to call lay people into the administrative leadership of the Church. If having fewer priests calls for bigger and fewer parishes, and if we move to a "big box" approach, as is often seen in the US, or to a satellite approach, we obviously need an array of lay experts who must be professional in their approach to what a parish is and to their part in it. So there does seem to be openness to subsidiarity together, with more need for standard diocesan protocols for lay leadership in administering. But does our understanding of lay participation also admit that lay people share somehow in the missionary roles of teaching, making holy and leading, as the Second Vatican Council taught?

What has become of the promise of lay participation, especially through parish and diocesan pastoral councils, as encouraged by Vatican II? Has such participation fallen on hard times? Do lay people truly have a place at the table as we grapple with the modern mission of the Church? Unless I am mistaken, pastors and bishops are feeling less committed to increasing levels of lay participation. Vatican II's vision of the central role of the laity in our Church has yet to be realized, probably in large part due to the tensions arising as a proper relationship between clergy and laity evolves. We remain distant from the vision of the Second Vatican Council that claimed the mission of the Church was not only to bring to men and women the message of Christ and his grace, but through the laity to penetrate and perfect the temporal sphere with the spirit of the gospel.

Religious Illiteracy

In his award-winning book *John A: The Man Who Made Us*, a biography of John A. Macdonald, Canada's first prime minister, Richard Gwyn speaks of the need for Canadians to know their own history. "Our history," he says, "... lacks the drama of revolutions and civil wars, of kings and queens losing their heads. But it is our history. It is us. It's where we came from and, in far larger part than often recognized, it is why we are the way we are now, no matter all the transformational changes since – demographic, economic, technological, life style."

Given the importance of knowing one's history, it is distressing to face another reality confronting the Catholic community: our young people, as generous and as altruistic as ever, do not know the story of our faith, the great meta-narrative that tells us who we are as believing people. They may be much better educated, but they are too often illiterate as far as the Catholic and Christian story is concerned.

Many young people in Catholic secondary schools betray an obvious lack of familiarity with the Eucharist, how to participate in it, and how to comport themselves. They lack a sense of the sacred and of a conceptual context within which to place the Eucharist as the centre of our Catholic life. Catholic elementary school students do not understand fundamental questions such as the nature and meaning of sacraments, and how sacraments have been traditionally understood in the life of the Church. This religious illiteracy may be partly due to a failure by schools, but mainly it is the effect of children growing up in families where faith is hardly practised, is seldom celebrated, and is given little practical importance. This situation is often exacerbated by the different priorities held by priests and by educators in Catholic schools.

Yet while many young people seem unfamiliar with the doctrinal teaching of the Christian tradition, they often have an impressive commitment to what Christians are called to do for the poor and marginalized.

The Search for God

Standing over and against this somewhat bleak picture is one of the most hopeful realities visible in both secular society and in the Church. Paradoxically, there are many indications of a contemporary search for God, or at least for a vision that will deepen the meaning of life. The fascination with spirituality is so much a part of our times. Amidst the humbling of the Church, the aggressiveness of the secularists, and faltering Catholic practice and credibility, there remains as a dominant feature of our times a pervasive search for God – or at least for the spiritual side of life – in ways both conscious and unconscious. The words of former Beatle George Harrison reflect the urgency of this seeking: "Everything else can wait, but the search for God cannot wait," he said. Canadian sociologist Reginald Bibby's ongoing surveys indicate an increase in participation in Church life in Canada.

But of greater significance are other signs of the times found in popular culture. The ongoing and ever more pointed spiritual search is found, for example, in the writings of the hugely popular Canadian author Douglas Coupland. From his bestselling *Generation X* to *Life After God* and, more recently, *Hey Nostradamus!*, one hears the recurrent theme of the emptiness of life without God.

In the popular poet and songwriter Leonard Cohen's CD *Ten New Songs*, he talks about "Boogie Street." "Boogie

Street" is Cohen's synonym for life. He writes and sings, "There's no one who has told us yet/ What Boogie Street is for."

Like people of every age, our society wants to know, has to know, what "Boogie Street" is for. In bookstores, countless titles try to tell us what life is for. Everything from the many variations on New Age Mysticism to *The Celestine Prophecy*, *The Da Vinci Code* and even *The Secret* betray a quest for something beyond possessions and material wealth.

Unfortunately, perhaps, many of these spiritual self-help tomes seek to lead the individual to find meaning in life only within the self. Yet for many, part of today's search for meaning involves a quest to discover one's origins, particularly in the family. More and more people today want to discover some coherent and consistent sense of meaning and direction within their families, their ancestors, their history, their story. This is the "Roots" phenomenon. Among other things, it reveals that meaning cannot be found in the self alone.

This latter phenomenon likely comes about because many people today sense a lack of continuity in their lives. The boilerplate determinism of modernity can leave behind a people whose story has been so deconstructed and relativized that they appear to be nothing of significance, to be hardly worthwhile. Intuitively, we know that it is our story, our history, that gives some sense of direction, some wonder and meaning, some importance to our personal lives. Without a story, a history, we feel that the human journey has no meaning because it has no coherent sense of beginning or end.

At the Intercontinental Congress on Vocations in Montreal in 2002, Sister Marie Chin RSM spoke of the Aboriginal people of Australia, who have a practice of walking hundreds or even thousands of miles in a year, tracking the patterns that their ancestor gods have left on the landscape as they created the world and its occupants in the mythical time known as the "Dream Time." Apparently, as they walk through particular areas, they sing and chant the story describing the events that took place in Dream Time in that region. In recalling their deep stories, people everywhere find fundamental values, beliefs, ways of acting and inspiration that give meaning to their present. Our stories hold a transformative power that touches our soul and provides a framework for belief and hope and peace in the midst of the fears and uncertainties that trouble us. Thus, despite declining Church attendance and participation, we live in a moment when people everywhere are searching out their family and tribal stories to give meaning to their lives.

Our Clerical World

In this environmental scan, the most important question is where we priests find ourselves in the midst of our somewhat disjointed but wonderfully challenging times. What are the hallmarks of the clerical culture and environment in which we fulfill our ministry?

The first characteristic of our clerical culture is that we are a happy group. Monsignor Stephen Rossetti of the St. Luke Institute provides data from his survey of priests done from 2003 to 2005, as well as that done by the National Federation of Priests' Councils in the U.S. From the tone and tenor of these studies, and from his meetings with priests around the world, he concludes that most priests consider the priesthood to be a great life. "The large majority," he says, "are happy and grateful."

These and other surveys seem to indicate that, individually, we priests are very comfortable with ourselves and with the work we do. The data say we have a high level of job satisfaction. Some 88 per cent of priests say they would choose the priesthood again. Andrew Greeley, in *Priests: A Calling in Crisis*, reports that the level of job satisfaction among Roman Catholic priests is significantly higher than among other professionals, such as physicians, lawyers, college professors and Protestant clergy. In fact, 91 per cent, according to Greeley, would encourage another man to enter the priesthood, whereas only half of physicians would encourage others to become doctors. Strangely, the data also say we do not believe that all this is true of other priests. Those others, we believe, have a morale problem. What brief conclusions can we draw about what is happening in our clerical world?

Chapter 5 examines in greater detail the need for love and intimacy in the life of a priest. Here, however, it deserves mention that the celibate life, by definition, carries with it a dimension of solitary living that can be unhealthy from both a spiritual and a psychological viewpoint. Most of us have long understood the distinction between the loneliness that distances us from others and the necessary solitude that provides a unique place for God in our lives. Loneliness is almost a structural threat to the priest's life. Not surprisingly, priests have always tended to hang together and establish firm and life-giving friendships with each other. That there are fewer and fewer priests means that, especially in rural areas, such friendships are more difficult to achieve and maintain.

Implicit in this natural seeking for clerical friendship is the danger of establishing friendships only with fellow priests, and distancing ourselves from the people to whom we minister. We risk creating and sustaining a clerical caste, reinforcing the clericalism mentioned earlier. Despite this caveat, let me underline the value and necessity of friendship and sharing of ministry among priests.

One of the encouraging realities of recent years has been the different kinds of coming together of priests to offer strength and support, and simply spend time together. This is not a new phenomenon, but one that seems to have gained momentum in the last few years. For example, rectories throughout North America have welcomed and consolidated living arrangements for priests from a number of parishes. In some cases, these priests cooperatively provide pastoral services for a region. In other cases, they simply share this common living arrangement and provide fraternity and support as they care for their different parishes. Priests are socializing together again, gathering of an afternoon or evening simply to enjoy each other's company, talking and reflecting on the latest baseball and hockey scores along with their pastoral tasks in the places they serve. Those best described as Lone Rangers remain, but as we will discuss later, a sense of presbyterate, of shared priesthood, seems to be growing.

And yet, when we gather for meetings and other occasions, certain things hit us hard. We talk about the decreasing levels of religious and sacramental practice; the lack of vocations to the priesthood and religious life, with the consequent greying of the clergy; the shame of clergy sexual abuse; problems of credibility, especially with the moral teaching of the Church; a lack of transparency in the Church; the distance between some young and some older priests; and the religious illiteracy of the younger generations.

In the last 50 years, priests in their seminary and continuing education have experienced revolutions in our understanding of scripture, theology and our own spiritual life. In a short space of time, we have gone from living in a Catholic world in which doubt was a sin – although we skirted that problem with the saying "a thousand difficulties don't make a doubt" – to realizing that we are confronted daily with questions of faith that plague our lives as never before. They are not as much questions of doubt as faithful questions. Anyone who has studied theology and scripture in the last four or five decades realizes that there is no going back from theology that takes into account the historical dimension, and most of us have benefited from the new insights of exploring scripture with the aid of the historical-critical method.

In the foreword to his 2007 book *Jesus of Nazareth*, Pope Benedict outlined the dangers if this latter approach becomes an exclusive one. At the same time, he accepts the value of this tool in deepening our knowledge of the scriptures. His book, which resulted from this historical-critical approach, may well be the most profound and spiritual examination of the meaning of Jesus of Nazareth that has come out of Rome in many years. Most priests these days would share Benedict XVI's approach to both theology and scripture working from the sacred writings and tradition of the Church without falling into fundamentalism. Doing theology is an exercise of their faith ever seeking deeper understanding.

The face of the Church, the people of God, has changed since I was ordained in 1960. Those to whom we preach on Sunday morning have many and more varied experiences of life and are much better educated than people used to be. The tumultuous events that began with the Second Vatican Council have helped the people in the pews realize that they, together with the deacon, priest or bishop, are the Church. The explosion of information and communications found amidst the multiplicity of television channels and the Internet have provided people with widely diverging opinions on everything from HIV/AIDS to genetic engineering to the variety of religious beliefs to population control. The authoritative voice of the magisterium is not the only authoritative voice that is heard. In this time of transition in the life of the Church and society, it seems clear that although we priests – and those to whom we minister – may believe a lot less about some of the minutiae associated with the Catholic religion, we also know a lot more about the message of the scriptures. We have learned in new and deeper fashion about the mystery and wonder of a creation that finds its origin in God, more about the interconnectedness of all reality, more about the ongoing reality of redemption and healing and salvation, and more about the wonderful holiness of so many people we meet in our ministry.

We have not lost or changed our minds about the God of creation, about his Son Jesus as the way, and about the Holy Spirit, who dwells within us. We still confess that "The crucified son of God is risen from the dead to give us his Holy Spirit." But we live in a world in which ideas are shifting even faster than the effects of climate change. We stand in that in-between space between a fairly static view of life and reality and a world that is dealing with information overload. In a Church that, for many years, had little time for doubt, it seems that now, for many, there are nothing but questions. The language we use to express our faith does not seem to have the same transforming power it once had, and so we look for new words, a new vocabulary. Within the last few decades we have all become somewhat familiar with microprocessors, laser beams, cloning, bio-engineering, gene therapy and other new technologies, but our ethical and religious fix on these realities has yet to catch up with many of these advances.

Nor have we got our minds around the immensity of the universe as revealed by the Hubble telescope and the NASA space program. New to humankind is the amazing relatedness of all reality, from the smallest quark, neutrino and photon to the newly discovered galaxies as revealed by particle scientists and astrophysicists respectively.

We wonder if our knowledge has outrun our faith – if we find ourselves with too much knowledge and too little understanding. At the same time, through this increased knowledge, most of us priests have in some way touched and been touched and have come to know more of the God within us and maybe less of the God who is remote from daily life. As we have moved beyond the image of God as puppeteer, as potentate, as judge or as prosecutor, we may have less difficulty in answering an oft-posed and pastorally difficult question: "Why did God let this happen to me, to you, to my family?"

As we look to Jesus, we are confronted as never before by the question he puts to all of us time and time again: "Who do you say I am?" We have not forgotten a theology that tells us of Jesus as Saviour and Redeemer – a theology that tells us at what cost Jesus has brought us back to the Father and to one another, from whom we had wandered in sin and weakness. But we have also deepened our personal understanding of Jesus as a brother – a brother whose life is not so much about paying some debt or ransom to the Father as it is about buying us back from forces deep within that often prove too powerful for us to resist by ourselves. In other words, through Jesus, God took the

initiative to remake humanity, including our own humanity, and thereby make all of us more human.

Theologically, we have embraced various definitions
and descriptions of our ministry. Some may remember a
teaching that described the priest as *alter Christus* – another
Christ, particularly in terms of the celebration of the sacraments. More recently, particularly in John Paul II's writings,
the emphasis has been on our ministry as acting *in persona
Christi*, in the person of Christ. We have come to realize
that we do not belong on pedestals, and that the people
we serve share the priestly, prophetic and kingly roles; we
are chosen from among them. Attempts to describe our
ministry raise the question of identity. Just who are we as
priests? How we answer this question obviously affects
how we understand ourselves, how we identify ourselves.
With Isaiah and Jeremiah, we believe we are called by God
in a special way – but called to be what? Are we leaders
or facilitators? Are we servants or the "main man"? At liturgy. are we the celebrant or the presider? When priestly
identity is threatened, we may be tempted to fade away or
to assert our clerical superiority. So some react by saying
that we are no more or less, no different than the people to
whom we minister. Others react by going out and buying
a biretta and a new soutane.

Perhaps even more disturbing to many priests is that,
at least at a superficial level, we don't always believe the
same thing. In-between times can be anxious times, and
some fairly strange behaviours can happen during them,
some of them our own. There can be more choosing of

sides, or polarization, than usual. Differences can create rifts and gulfs between priests who are part of the same presbyterate, who are brothers in the priesthood, serving the same Lord in the same diocese.

To know the history of the Church is to know that from the Acts of the Apostles to the present day, a variety of theological opinions have emerged in this Church of ours. Whatever interpretation we give to our Creed, our doctrine and our scriptures, we all accept that they carry for us the ideas and understandings that underlie our Christian life and spirituality. To put it another way, we share that the mystery of our individual and collective lives focuses upon a creating and loving and sustaining God; that Jesus is the way to him; that the Holy Spirit lives in each of us and in all of us together; and that this Church of ours, the people of God, is the great sign and sacrament of God acting within this world of his creation.

We live, nonetheless, as the Benedictine nun Joan Chittister says, "in a desert between two places." Or perhaps it is better to say that we speak and hear two languages: the language of faith and the unbelieving and increasingly antagonistic language of secularism. And we look for new words that will bridge the gulf.

The concluding paragraphs of *Presbyterorum Ordinis*, Vatican II's document on the priesthood, point out that despite the joys that can accompany this vocation, priests will have moments when they feel "like strangers in this world"; when they can be struck by "the seeming sterility of their past labours and also the bitter loneliness" which "can lead them to the danger of becoming depressed in spirit" (para. 22).

One of the metaphors often used in the years immediately following Vatican II was that like God's chosen people in their Exodus experience, we must wander in the desert as we search for a new way of being Church. This metaphor has sometimes painfully hit home in recent years. One thing is clear: we seem to know as never before what the desert really is! If, in our various environments, we seem to be in the desert, if at times we appear to be in exile, it helps to remember that it was in these new lands, in this exile, that the Lord worked the transformation of his people.

No matter how we describe and understand the various environments in which we live, few would deny that we need to have hope. This hope appears to be alive and well in our presbyterate. In the following chapter, I will reflect upon the hope that is ours and that is the bridge over the troubled waters of our times. As priests, we also need certainty about the distinctive spirituality that is ours. We need a deepened sense of obedience and solidarity with the bishop, with the diocese and with one another. We need as well to ever plumb anew the depths of how we love as Christians and as priests. And we must look to the future. These topics will be explored in the following chapters.

$\mathcal{S}$ustained by Hope

Each time Catholics gather to celebrate Eucharist, we pray and speak of ourselves as people who "wait in joyful hope for the coming of our Saviour, Jesus Christ."

Many today find in our society a prevailing uneasiness about what the future holds. We worry about global warming and climate change spiralling out of control, as the ice caps melt and tornadoes multiply. We see finite energy sources being seriously depleted. We are concerned about having enough food for the world as populations grow and genetically modified foods threaten the control of food production. Terrorism, we have learned, looms just around the corner. The economic uncertainties of a severe recession leave many profoundly anxious about their financial future. Some are filled with dread about what is happening around them – a dread that is almost too deep to name and to face.

Despite the rays of hope we glimpsed in reviewing our social, ecclesial and clerical cultures, the people we serve, and we ourselves, feel the lurking uncertainty. We may unconsciously fear that emptiness will prevail. Many can identify with the words of Woody Allen in the film *Annie Hall*: "God is dead, Marx is dead … and I don't feel too well myself!"

Priests who work in parishes are at the front lines of the people of God, the Church. Parishioners look to us for hope. We are expected to speak a word that reveals God's presence when we celebrate the baptisms, weddings, anniversaries and other moments that serve as milestones in the lives of parishioners. They especially look to us for a word of hope when they and their loved ones face sickness, death and other tragedies. Even within our own ranks, when malaise, burnout, fatigue, disillusionment and other ills arise, we seek hope in our lives and in our vocation to the priesthood.

We do live each day very aware of the practical effects of a severely reduced number of colleagues in the priesthood. This situation has several implications beyond the lack of manpower in our parishes.

- It means that families do not encourage their sons to embrace this vocation to which we have given our lives. When we look over our shoulders, we discover that no one is following.

- It suggests that what we do is unimportant. Some men left the priesthood in the last three or four decades when they realized that priests were no longer admired by society. Indeed, many people, including Catholics, now view priests with suspicion. Catholicism and its priests are often the butt of a malicious humour that would not be tolerated elsewhere in these politically correct times. If it is true that the only intellectually accepted bigotry is anti-Catholicism, then parish priests, as the most visible representatives of Roman Catholicism, are directly in the line of fire.

- As we look around at our contemporaries at every deanery meeting, we are ever more aware of the thin grey line we priests have become. An increasing number of us are approaching the finish line in this great pilgrimage called life. Many of us are definitely playing the back nine.

Only men of hope can continue to sustain their morale and, perhaps even more importantly, present the face of hope to those we serve. Reflecting on hope in our lives has never been more urgent.

The priest shares in the prophetic ministry of the bishop of the diocese. The prophet is called not so much to talk about the future as to discern the meaning of the present. The priest as prophet is called to find meaning, to give hope in and beyond all the life situations that we and those we serve must face.

Margaret Somerville, the Canadian ethicist, says that all humans must actively engage in realistic "hope making." She describes human hope as "the oxygen of the human spirit; without it," she says, "our spirit dies; with it we can overcome even seemingly insurmountable obstacles." That hope is a habit of the heart, a virtue. This virtue of hope is the promise and the guarantee that "we can face our present," as Pope Benedict says in his 2007 encyclical on hope, *Spe Salvi*.

The First Letter of Peter is addressed to pagan or Gentile converts to the Church in its early days. They are people who appear to be living in an alien and hostile environment. Although it was not a time of state persecution, these early Christians were being harassed and relegated to the fringes of society. Not unlike today, being a Christian was a challenge. The author of First Peter seeks to encourage them with his very first words. He reminds them of who they are: people whom God has given "a new birth into a living hope through the resurrection of Jesus Christ from the dead, and into an inheritance that is imperishable, undefiled, and unfading" (1 Peter 1:3-4). In chapter 3, the author tells his readers that despite their difficulties and suffering, they are called to "have your answer ready for people who ask you for the reason for the hope that you all have." We priests are likewise called to give reason for the hope we all have within us, as fragile as it may be at times.

As we seek the hope that will sustain us today, the letters of Paul offer great consolation and information.

He has much to say about the hope that sustains us and strengthens our faith.

When our hope seems in short supply, one source of strength is surely the letter to the Philippians. Here, Paul is writing from prison or house arrest. Despite the series of events that have overtaken him – beatings, jailings, narrow escapes, shipwrecks, and other crises – he writes these words to the Philippians: "I thank my God every time I remember you, constantly praying with joy in every one of my prayers for all of you, because of your sharing in the gospel ..." (1:3-5). He adds, "I want you to know, beloved, that what has happened to me has actually helped to spread the gospel" (1:12). Continuing, Paul exhorts the Philippians, "If then there is any encouragement in Christ, any consolation from love, any sharing in the Spirit, any compassion and sympathy, make my joy complete: be of the same mind, having the same love, being in full accord and of one mind" (2:1-2). In Philippians, one hears echoes of the people "who wait in joyful hope," as we pray in the Eucharist, after the Our Father. It is an epistle marked by exuberance and a zest for life – a joyful hope and ministry that belies the fact that Paul is getting old and creaky. Philippians suggests that we can practise our ministry with great good humour that speaks of people who are sure that they are loved by God and by one another. It may have been Philippians that inspired a theologian and holy man of our time, Gustavo Gutierrez, to write that "what God does best and most is trust us with our moment in history." This is our moment. Hope helps us trust that we are good for it – we can do it.

Paul speaks of hope more specifically as he writes to the little, struggling Christian community in Rome. He promises his readers that they will have peace with God through Jesus (Rom. 5:1ff) if they are steadfast. He goes on to say that "we also boast in our sufferings," for "suffering produces endurance, and endurance produces character, and character produces hope, and hope does not disappoint us, because God's love has been poured into our hearts through the Holy Spirit that has been given to us" (Rom. 5:3-5).

In chapter 4 of Romans, Paul puts forward Abraham as a great figure of faith and hope and trust in God. Of Abraham he says, "Hoping against hope, he believed that he would become 'the father of many nations' ..." (4:18).

We have much to learn from Abraham these days. Our review of our social, ecclesial and clerical environments reminds us that, like Abraham and his wife Sarah, we have been called from the certainties and security of our ministry to a new land that seems less than benign. We experience today not so much a sense of despair, but a disturbing lack of the sureness of another day. Our ministry can at times seem ill fated. Despite our best efforts, our preaching of the gospel – at least at first blush – seems to have little obvious effect. When we priests gather and greet each other around the table we can see that, like Abraham, we have become old and grey. Like him, we carry on sustained by a promise: that our work will bear fruit, and that new life, a great nation, a holy people will spring forth from our ministry.

So what is this hope that we are called to rely on, to stir up, to give witness to for the sake of the people to whom we preach the gospel? What is this hope that the letter to the Hebrews encourages us to grasp? This letter invites us to "seize the hope set before us" – hope that is the "anchor of the soul" (Heb. 6:18-19).

The *Catechism of the Catholic Church*, meanwhile, tells us that "Hope is the theological virtue by which we desire the kingdom of heaven and eternal life as our happiness, placing our trust in Christ's promises and relying not on our own strength, but on the help of the grace of the Holy Spirit" (para. 1817). Speaking about this virtue in *Spe Salvi*, Pope Benedict tells us that our hope in a promised future changes the present. "The present," he says, "is touched by the future reality, and thus the things of the future spill over into those of the present and those of the present into those of the future" (para. 7). With apologies to the systematic theologians, I confess that although I know faith and hope have different formal objects, they have always seemed rather the same to me. Through both of them, we recognize that somehow we have been gifted with the baptismal power of the Spirit, gifted with the capability of trusting ultimately not in ourselves but in the God whose face has been revealed in Jesus of Nazareth.

The hope that sustains us, Joan Chittister says in wonderfully poetic language, "... stands rooted in the certainties of the future hinted at by the past but yet unaccomplished. Hope whispers within us," she says, "like a soft steady draft of daylight that what we believe in we shall attain. Hope leads us around the dark corners looking for the grace of the moment, confident that God's will for us is good."

More analytically and less poetically, we recognize that hope is not optimism. Over the years, most of us have come to realize the distinction between the two. There are things that happen that we just can't be optimistic about.

Optimism is foreseeing the eventual positive outcome of the problems and difficulties that beset us. We may either feel optimistic or pessimistic that problems in the Middle East will soon be resolved, vocations will increase, people will come back to Mass, collections will rise, and Rome and the bishop will finally get it right!

Hope, on the other hand, does not pretend to know the answer or outcome, yet trusts and believes. Abraham is the great figure of hope. In an essay entitled "Journeying in Hope," the English Roman Catholic theologian Nicholas Lash writes,

> Abraham knew i) where he came from: from his own land and his father's house. And ii) he knew why he was journeying: in obedience to God's command. And iii) he knew that this journey in obedience to God's command was a necessary condition for the realization of God's promise, the promise that he would in a new and better land, be made into a 'great nation' sustained and cherished by God.

Lash goes on to suggest that even in his trust and hope and faith, Abraham did not know where he was going. He trusted and believed despite the fact that there was a disturbing bleakness to his pilgrimage.

In hope there is a certain acceptance of dispossession. We accept that we cannot predict the outcome of where God leads us. All that illumines our way is the knowledge of where we have come from and where we are ultimately destined. Hope, then, is journeying when we do not have the answer or the outcome. All we have is the promise, like Abraham and Sara had – a promise that they would be the father and mother of a great nation.

The great Cardinal Newman had words that shed light on the meaning of Christian hope. He described it as accepting and living with a "veil over futurity."

The Book of Jeremiah recounts the story of a prophet who surely must have wished on more than one occasion that he had been called to be a bank teller or a taxi driver or a miner or a land surveyor rather than to God's ministry of prophecy. Around the year 600 BCE, God called Jeremiah to announce an unpopular message. His contemporaries were all for sidling up to their Egyptian neighbours and using a political and military alliance to throw off the oppressive yoke of the Babylonians, who ruled the Middle East. Jeremiah rejected this approach and was ridiculed for his efforts. He was persecuted, put in the stocks in the city square, and thrown in jail. The word of God that he preached found very little resonance, echoing only faintly among a people who were looking for a very different message. Poor old Jeremiah! He had little scope for optimism.

But Jeremiah did not need optimism, for ultimately he was a man filled with hope. He knew that when God speaks, his ministers, his prophets, must listen. As in Jeremiah's time, the Spirit of God urges today's ministers to go and speak to God's people. Like Jeremiah. we have to go. Despite the sounds of the at times seductive music that surrounds us, we know that there is a right way to act and live. We know that we have come forth from the mystery of God and journey in life back to the fullness of this mystery. What is clear from Jeremiah's story is that there is meaning beyond the moment that grabs us and tempts us. When we feel that life would be more bearable if we simply enjoyed the party, a more profound world view reminds us to tune into the frequency of God. We know that light shines even in darkness and eventually replaces darkness. We know that the message of hope in Jeremiah and, even more so, that of the Book of Revelation, reveal a God of wonder and mystery. This God assures us that good will triumph.

Job, too, offers us a sign of hope. Although we often speak of someone having the patience of Job, the Book of Job tells a story not about patience, but about hope. This hope is based not on short-term outcomes but on a vision of life and ultimate trust in God. As Job's universe crashes down around him, as his vision of what life will mean for him is rudely taken away, as all the things he finds meaning in disappear, as all the support of family vanishes – when nothing in his life allows for optimism – Job, despite his impatience with both God and friends, remains a man of hope. In the refrain we use so often in the funeral liturgy at the final commendation, we hear an adaptation of Job's words:

> For I know that my Redeemer lives,
>> and that at the last he will stand upon the earth;
> and after my skin has been thus destroyed,
>> then in my flesh I shall see God. (Job 19:25-26)

In her little book *Mystical Hope*, Episcopalian priest Cynthia Bourgeault talks of the hope we find in the scriptures. This kind of hope is not based on good outcomes – a biopsy that reveals no cancer, a miraculous intervention, a fuller church or better collections than last year. Rather, this hope is based on trust in the mercy of God. As an example, she points out that towards the end of the Book of Habakkuk, the prophet, after a long litany of doom and gloom, suddenly cries out,

> Though the fig tree does not blossom,
>> and no fruit is on the vines;
> though the produce of the olive fails
>> and the fields yield no food;
> though the flock is cut off from the fold
>> and there is no herd in the stalls,
> yet I will rejoice in the Lord;
>> I will exult in the God of my salvation. (3:17-18)

What one sees in the lives of Abraham and Jeremiah and Job and Habakkuk offers us a hopeful way of being. In them we recognize a relationship with God, a way of living that our theology has traditionally called "habitual grace" or "the state of grace," the sanctifying grace or dynamic of life into which we are baptized. This, ultimately, is the "surround sound" of the Christian life, the Spirit of God within us and around us. In this state, hope is one of the central habits of the heart or virtues that shape our understanding, our grasp of, and our attitude towards life itself and the existence which we share. That vision allows us to perceive, however dimly, that we and the energy and love that is God are one.

What I am trying to say here is that if we believe in our baptism – and the grace of our ordination – then because of our graced existence, the waters we swim in, the primordial environment that surrounds and shapes us, is the grace of God's life. This conviction provides the sustaining hope that leads us ever forward in life, even if we don't always know where we are going.

In her book, Cynthia Bourgeault recounts the medieval legend of the Irish St. Brendan:

> Brendan sets out to search for the Land Promised to the Saints. But for seven years he keeps missing it – keeps sailing around in circles. He can find it only when something is reversed inside him. Instead of looking outward for landfalls and destinations, an inner eye opens within Brendan that can see the luminous fullness of the Land Promised to the Saints always and

everywhere present beneath the surface motions of coming, going, striving, and arriving.

He discovers the grace and the hope that is within him. To find our way to that visionary world, to that fullness at the heart of everything, is the journey straight to the wellsprings of what Bourgeault calls mystical hope.

If there is any virtue that all believers, and surely priests, cannot do alone, it is hope. We must turn to one another. We cannot hope alone. We must give hope to one another. This surely means that we flee cynicism, which is the morass in which hope suffocates. This doesn't mean that we will not laugh uproariously at some of the lunacies that sometimes issue from our own mouths, the mouths of confreres, and even the mouths of those who should know better. But we will refuse to sink into the quicksand of never expecting better. We will refuse to sit quietly in the company of those who take pleasure in raining on every parade in our society, in our Church and in our presbyterate.

One hears a range of professions or confessions of the beliefs that sustain people these days. In the summer of 2007, CBC Radio ran a series called "This I Believe," where a number of Canadians recounted the significant beliefs that gave inspiration to their lives. Catholic Christians, and indeed all Christians, should be able to look to their ministers to profess a belief that might go something like this:

We believe as Christians and we have hope because we know the end of the story, and it is a happy ending:

eternal life in the utter bliss of God. We believe how blessed we are to live in this ongoing story and the hope it offers. We believe that because we can face death with hope, then we can live life much more generously, bringing to those we serve the vision of caring life that the gospel announces.

There will always be, however, a temptation to live on the surface of that mystery, to act as though the power that lives in us through Jesus' death and resurrection fixes things, guarantees our success, or at least allows us to hunker down and wait out the bad times with our eyes shut. But in real life, we know that some things don't get fixed; some things we desperately pray for don't happen; that certain evils we pray against occur anyway. And we recognize all too well that despite vocation campaigns and prayers for vocations to the priesthood, we still find ourselves going to more priests' funerals than ordinations.

Despite God's marvellous interventions on behalf of God's people, as described in the Hebrew scriptures, we know that over a long period of time, they came to grasp that the Lord was not a God of quick fixes. Yet we also know that they, and we, never really get over the temptation to make of God some kind of magician and problem solver rather than the ultimate mystery of our existence. If we are honest with ourselves, we admit that we are pretty attached to these hoped-for outcomes for which we plan and pray and work; to a great extent, we base our hope upon them. When they do not materialize as we expected, when the long haul becomes a very long haul, it takes a special kind of faith and courage to keep announcing a word of hope. That is why, I suppose, we must ever strive to uncover that deeper hope that is in us, that is the very ground of our being. As Sister Veronica O'Reilly says, this hope allows us to continue prophesying and loving and serving our God and our human community.

James Carroll, the novelist and former priest, speaking after the death of the great Protestant minister and social activist William Sloane Coffin, said,

> In the choices he made, and in the language he used, Bill Coffin held up the possibility of hope. He proclaimed by his preaching and his living that the human heart is not doomed to break, however cracked it is by war, by injustice, or even by the sorrows, say, of a child who dies too young. To the mystification and even consternation of many, Bill Coffin defined himself by Jesus. And what did Bill love about Jesus, if not the paradox? The contradictions that added up to hope. Jesus, the peasant nobody who is Lord of the universe. Jesus, the victim who is victorious. Jesus, who can say, "My God, my God, why have You abandoned me?" while also saying, "Into Your hands."

On a more mundane level, when I think of some of the ways in which, as an ordained leader, my humanity has gotten in the way of my responsibility, and yet still witness the wonderful ways the Lord uses me for others, I realize that God's power is far stronger than my own limitations. This I find immensely hopeful. In some incomplete way, it seems to acknowledge a great force field of divine energy moving always toward the good – a great force field of love and compassion in which I am immersed. When we apprehend this mystery, allow ourselves to enter into its depths in contemplation, gently and gradually let go of specific outcomes, and let go of our fear of dying and diminishment, we are carried by this energy into the future, into new ways of becoming and acting.

In his book *Jesus of Nazareth*, Pope Benedict speaks of the Sermon on the Mount as a teaching that turns the world upside down. The Sermon on the Mount speaks to the paradox that is Christianity. It speaks of our true environment – the environment of the waters of God's love and energy in which we live and move and have our being. It speaks of a hope that dares us to keep turning our world upside down.

This hope enlightens even in our darkest moments. With Joan Chittister we can recall that "When Jesus died, hope died. The apostles grieved the death of Jesus. The public was scandalized. The synagogues said good riddance to a troublemaker. The entire enterprise collapsed. But in the end, out of apparent failure, came new life stronger than it had ever been before."

Such is the virtue, the habit of the heart, that is hope – a contemporary virtue for priests, if ever there was one. With it we will indeed continue to lead our parishioners to "wait in joyful hope for the coming of our Saviour, Jesus Christ."

$\mathcal{T}$he Distinctive Spirituality of the Diocesan Priest

The search for God, or at least the quest for some kind of spirituality, is a hallmark of our modern or post-modern Western society. Some thinkers, such as the great German theologian Karl Rahner, insist that if spirituality is to sustain a person in these secular times, it must dare to approach the mysticism that lies at the heart of Christian spirituality.

If this is true for society in general, then priests are doubly in need of an ever-deepening spirituality. In the last two or three decades we have been wounded in various ways, sometimes by our own hand, and we practise a ministry that has been marginalized in the eyes of many. Priests, not surprisingly, seek to deepen their spirituality and to strengthen their vocational commitment and resolve – not only to serve themselves, but to serve those who turn to them. Many Catholics – and others as well – turn to the priest not always aware of their quest for an integrating belief that they suspect will provide a deeper direction and meaning to their lives. They are looking for holiness, and holiness is what the Church is all about.

Today, many in the priesthood and in religious life have sought to make more explicit their own identity and the identity of their profession and vocation. They have sought to clarify the charism, the particular gift God has given to them, both collectively and individually, to fulfill their religious calling. Religious communities in particular, as they examine their present involvements and lifestyles and search out their roots, seek to better understand the gift of the Spirit that underlies their ministry in the world.

The Sisters of St. Joseph, for example, have worked for decades in health care, education, music and the arts, social justice and social welfare, and spiritual direction. More recently, they have come to recognize that inspiring all of these apostolates is a distinctive charism: an urging from God's Spirit towards a ministry of reconciling and unifying division in Church and society. They recognize that as a community, in and through their several ministries or apostolates, they are called in a special way to shorten the many distances that separate people, whether they be believers or non-believers, affluent or poor, liberals or conservatives, marginalized or entitled.

Many diocesan or secular priests ask, "What is *our* particular charism? Do we even have one?" The best answer I have heard to that question is that the charism of secular priests is to make their parishioners holy, to introduce depth and integrity into human lives. In the Book of Leviticus, the Lord reveals to Moses that before all else, the Lord called this people to himself; they are to enter into his holiness. "Speak to all the congregation of the people of Israel and say to them: You shall be holy, for I the Lord your God am holy" (19:1-2). *Lumen Gentium*, Vatican II's dogmatic constitution on the Church, underlines the essential call to holiness of every Christian. This important document teaches that "all the faithful of Christ of whatever rank or status are called to the fullness of the Christian life and to the perfection of charity" (para. 40). "'All of Christ's followers," it says, "are invited and bound to pursue holiness and the perfect fulfillment of their proper state" (para. 42).

By virtue of their ordination, priests share in the bishop's threefold ministry of guiding, teaching and sanctifying or making holy. Priests *guide* those they serve and *teach* them so that they can move surely on the path to *holiness*. Our fellow believers seek integrity, wholeness and a sense of the sacred that gives ultimate meaning to all they do. They want to realize all that they can become, to complete and live up to what they sense lives deep within them. They might not use the word "holiness," but they want to be holy, and they want their priests to guide and assist them in this search. This conclusion may seem simplistic, but I believe it contains a profound truth. It suggests that, more than ever, we as priests are realizing that our own spirituality, our own path to holiness, is intimately related to our mission and charism of helping the people we serve become holy. In this area, priests must be specialists. As John Paul II said in his visit to Poland in 2006, "The faithful expect only one thing from priests, that they be specialists in promoting the encounter between man and God."

The priest's primary ministry is to preach the word of God and to celebrate God's sacramental activity. Both of these actions are the foundation stones of a ministry of making holy, of assisting our parishioners to enter more deeply into the life of God. The patriarchs of old transmitted to the people the blessings of God and the blessings of life; it is no accident that asking the priest for a blessing is very much a part of our Catholic tradition. After all, a blessing is given to make something holy or, to put it a better way, to bring out the holiness in the many facets of the human journey. Newly ordained priests are asked for their blessing. As part of a priest's visit, Catholics welcome a blessing on their family. In the hospital, patients look to us to bless them. Our people ask us to bless their homes. They expect that in some way we will help to bring holiness into their lives, or reveal the holiness in their lives, and thereby assist in making them holy.

Presbyterorum Ordinis, Vatican II's document on the priesthood, contains a whole section entitled "The Priestly Call to Perfection." All Christians are aware of the scriptural basis for this call. In Matthew 5:48, Jesus says "we are to be perfect as our heavenly Father is perfect." Many feel intimidated by this call at first. It might help to park that notion in this discussion – to set it aside and speak of the priest's call to holiness rather than to perfection. Benedictine sister Joan Chittister claims that long ago, humankind fell victim to a most insidious form of spiritual arrogance – "the notion that there is such a thing as perfection and that humans are capable of achieving it."

In his poem "Anthem," Leonard Cohen suggests that we humans do well to engage life, acknowledging that there are cracks even in the best we can offer. However, he says that it is through the cracks that light gets in.

Perfection seems so presumptuous. If we are called to be perfect as our heavenly Father is perfect, then I think this means in the sense of being compassionate as our heavenly Father is compassionate. This we can strive for as we seek to share the passion of suffering, the passion of life, the passion of celebration, and the passion of love with those we serve. We do this as broken and sinful human beings embracing the broken and sinful human beings we serve. Striving for compassion is a surely a striving for holiness. In compassion, we share the journey of life together with people. We offer the peace that comes whenever we bear their burdens with them. We strive to help our parishioners bring together what is broken in their lives, to discover not just their weakness and sin, but their sacredness and integrity.

In fulfilling this ministry and task, the holiness of the priest is discovered, fostered and sustained. Through this compassion, he offers tangible hope and discovers a deepened hope in his own life. In this way, I believe, we ourselves embark upon and pursue the search for holiness. This holiness is often elusive, and sometimes tattered and imperfect. But it seems more attainable in our journey than perfection. The renowned Quaker educator Parker Palmer insists that "Wholeness [and holiness] does not mean perfection: [indeed] it means embracing brokenness as an integral part of life." Few priests have not heard and embraced that wonderfully realistic description of ourselves as "wounded healers." One of the reassuring prayers in our quest for holiness is found in the antiphon for the Magnificat for Thursday of Week Four in the Office: "If you hunger for holiness, God will satisfy your longing, good measure, and flowing over."

How, then, as diocesan priests, do we work at making ourselves and our parishioners holy? As we look back to the spiritual formation we received in the seminary, as good as it may have been for that era, it appears out of tune or out of sync with the calling and lifestyle of the diocesan priest today. In seminary days, we learned a spiritual regime as a way to holiness. It involved meditating early in the morning, praying the rosary and a visit to or adoration of the Blessed Sacrament, the practice of particular examen at noon, some spiritual reading throughout the day, the breviary said at prescribed times, general examen at night, and so on. After I was ordained, I was immediately posted as an assistant in a large and busy parish. The pace was frenetic. As the newest and youngest priest on staff, I took all the night calls from two general hospitals, a psychiatric hospital and elsewhere; was assigned a few groups of the Legion of Mary; visited a school or two; and was responsible for marriage preparation, convert instruction, regular hospital visits, early morning masses, and hearing lots of confessions (and not only on Saturday afternoons)! The regime I had learned in the seminary didn't fit. I was frustrated and feeling guilty for failing to follow the regime the seminary taught me. Luckily – or providentially – I had as a confessor a wise man, a religious, who early on said to me, "All those spiritual exercises to be accomplished at particular times don't work for your ministry." He suggested that given the lifestyle and uncertain schedule of the diocesan priest, finding some dedicated periods of time each week and each month to pray and reflect on what was going on in my ministry made more sense.

I suspect that the very pastoral US bishop Kenneth Untener was moving in the same direction when he commented that diocesan priests on retreat often make resolutions about how to fit spiritual exercises into a busy life. Better, Untener says, "to take the pattern that is there (if one can call our schedules a pattern) and find ways to build into it an attentiveness to God that runs from morning till night."

In recent years, we diocesan priests – at least we older ones – have come to realize that the spirituality we learned as seminarians, based on wonderful authors and spiritual guides such as Dom Marmion, Chautard, Dubay and even Tanquery, was derived from and exemplified monastic spirituality. This spirituality originated in the ordered days of men or women living in a monastic community where life was precisely arranged and organized, determined by the bells that summoned them to various moments of prayer 24 hours a day, 365 days a year.

In his book *What Are They Saying About the Ministerial Priesthood?* theologian Daniel Donovan says,

> The idea of a spirituality rooted in the pastoral ministry marks a shift from pre-conciliar emphases. The French school of spirituality tended to see the priest as a man set apart, *homo segregatus, dedicated* in a special way to a life of prayer and contemplation. The heart of his spiritual life was the sacrifice of the mass. The priest's task is to share in Christ's sacrifice by a life of prayer and self-denial. … This enormously influential spirituality was almost entirely conceived apart from any actual involvement in the pastoral ministry. It could be embraced by monk, religious, or parish priest.

Another bump on the road in our quest for a spirituality suited to our lives was the theological basis for our spirituality. Many of us first related to the concept of the priest as an *alter Christus* – another Christ who, particularly in his power to confect sacraments, stood above and apart from the lay people he ministered to. Likewise, he stood apart from them by living a different spirituality. Today, most see the priest as one of the People of God – a brother called to minister. The Spirit calls him from among his fellow believers to serve them as Christ would.

Today, we ask, "Is there a spirituality for the secular priest that is up to the task?" To explore this question, let us first look at spirituality in general.

Spirituality is much more than knowing how to pray – although prayer is an essential element. Rather, spirituality derives from the beliefs, attitudes, convictions and commitments from deep within us that determine our approach to life, to others and to God. It is about our heart, how we see things, how we feel things, and how these influence the way we live out our lives.

Widely varied spiritualities have abounded throughout the history of humankind. The apostle Paul spoke of radically different spiritualities when he wrote to the Christian community in Rome, "For those who live according to the flesh, set their minds on the things of the flesh, but those who live according to the Spirit set their minds on the things of the Spirit" (Rom. 8:5). In some way, spirituality is about how we free ourselves to be all that God created us to be.

In *The Holy Longing*, Ron Rolheiser paraphrases Plato, saying that "we are fired into life with a madness that comes from the gods, and which would have us believe that we can have a great love, perpetuate our own seed, and contemplate the divine." According to Rolheiser, everyone has a spirituality, whether it be life-giving or destructive. We all have this fire in our bellies. What we do with the fire is our spirituality. Spirituality, he says, "... is about being integrated or falling apart, about being community or being lonely, about being in harmony with Mother Earth or being alienated from her." Our spirituality, then, is about how we deal with the desires that are so much a part of our hearts.

More specifically, for the Christian, Richard McBrien writes, "To be spiritual means to know, and to live according to the knowledge that there is more to life than meets the eye." Christian spirituality, of course, is profoundly centred in the person of Jesus Christ, in commitment to him and to the meaning his message offers. This spirituality is rooted in Jesus' revelation to us of a God who is Father, Son and Spirit. As the First Letter of Peter makes clear, all that is revealed in the life, death and resurrection of Jesus is meant to lead us to God (3:18-19).

Christian spirituality, therefore, is founded on our belief in Jesus as the human face of God, and on the Spirit of God who dwells within us, within our community, and calls us ever closer to the mystery of God. It is a spirituality that insists, in Julian of Norwich's words, that "Love is the meaning of God."

Let us now return to the question of priests' spirituality. As diocesan priests, how do we express, practise and understand it? Is there an expression of Christian spirituality tailored for us diocesan priests? Is there a spirituality founded on our relationship with Jesus and through him with the Father and the Spirit that takes into account our ministry within a particular diocese and our relationships with the bishop, with other priests, and with lay people?

Lumen Gentium is the foundational document from Vatican II; all the other documents seem to flow from its vision of Church as, first and foremost, the people of God. Whatever distinctions exist between sacred ministers and the rest of the people of God, this document teaches that "Pastors and the *other* faithful are bound to each other by a mutual need" (para. 32). It also tells us that our lay brothers and sisters, although they have a special calling within the secular world, nonetheless seek to discover God deep within their hearts and lives. Together with the priests who serve them, they want to know more fully what it means to be God's people.

This seems to suggest that uncovering the spirituality of the diocesan priest requires us to acknowledge that there is indeed but one spirituality, which we share with every Christian. Our ministry is to help our fellow Christians in discovering and fostering this spirituality. In this way, our ministry assists them on the journey to holiness. The first Preface for Sundays in Ordinary Time tells us that *together* we are called to be a "chosen race, a royal priesthood, a holy nation, a people set apart." *Lumen Gentium* speaks of the call to holiness of the whole Church, in all its members (cf. paras. 39 and 41). Indeed, the Church is all about holiness, and priests seek to be guides on this inward journey. In a society that often militates against Christian life, the priest searches with his brothers and sisters to lead the "holy restlessness" of our souls towards adult faith.

Our spirituality, then, is grounded in the fact that we are priests taken from the people, who are the Church. We are called to serve our brothers and sisters who live in a secular world in their quest for holiness. But there is more to it: *our spirituality must arise out of our conversation with God about what we are doing in ministry to and for and with these people we serve.*

One of the prayers for the funeral of a priest reads, "Lord God, you chose our brother N. to serve your people as a priest and to share the joys and burdens of their lives." Ministering to the sick and hurting, the poor and abandoned; dealing with death and divorce, with families torn asunder; preparing homilies; administering the sacraments; sharing the joy of baptisms, weddings and anniversaries; enjoying fellowship at parties and barbecues; celebrating the wondrous feasts of Christmas and Easter – all these are the stuff of this spirituality. It has been described as sort of "street spirituality." We learn it and we learn from it as we figuratively and literally walk the streets where our parishioners live, accompanying them on their journeys. I clearly recall going to Mass in a parish where I had served as pastor. Not being needed to distribute communion I watched those approaching the table. Suddenly, I was struck by memories of my pastoral involvement in the lives of so many. I recognized the many dedicated parents; the wonderful teachers who taught me what Catholic schools were all about; the young girl who had been raped; the

couples whose lives were altered when their children became seriously ill; the single person who was lonely; the
recovering alcoholics; the families who had experienced
much pain as trust broke down; parents who had lost children; and the older woman who told me about climbing
into the hospital bed and holding her husband in her arms
as he died at four o'clock in the morning.

Perhaps the best example of how our spirituality arises
out of our ministry is seen in how we prepare our homilies.
Preaching is the first ministry of the bishop and of priests
who share his mission. In the gospels, the principal mission Jesus gives his disciples is to proclaim the kingdom of
God. *Presbyterorum Ordinis,* in describing the ministry and
the life of the priest, says, "... priests as co-workers with
their bishops, have as their *primary duty* the proclamation
of the gospel of God to all" (para. 4). In preaching we immerse ourselves in the word, in the sacred writings of the
people of God; at the same time, we immerse ourselves
in the lives of the people to whom we preach. We seek
to find a fit between their and our experiences of life and
the great story of the Bible and of the Church, which
gives meaning and direction to our lives. We pray to gain
insight into the readings we want to preach on, and we
reflect on the lives of those to whom we preach. To make
any progress, we must converse with God.

Most of us have heard often enough that the role of
the priest is *contemplata aliis tradere* – to hand on to others
what we have prayed about. Another way of saying this
is that only if we continually try to speak to God about

our ministry can we bring God's word to the women and men we serve. One can turn this dynamic around and still come up with the same dialectic. In *The Spirituality of the Diocesan Priest*, Donald Cozzens quotes the great Jewish rabbi Abraham Heschel, saying that maybe the *contemplata aliis tradere* is better understood as "We priests preach in order to pray; and that others might pray!"

Again, *Presbyterorum Ordinis* tells us, "As priests search for a better way to share with others the fruits of their own contemplation, they will win a deeper understanding of the 'unfathomable riches of Christ' (Eph. 3:8) as well as the manifold wisdom of God" (para. 13). In other words, as I understand it, this is the way of the spirituality of the diocesan priest. This same document says of us, "... by their everyday sacred actions themselves, as by the entire ministry which they exercise in union with the bishop and their fellow priests, they are being directed toward perfection of life" (para. 12). It adds, "Priests will attain sanctity in a manner proper to them if they exercise their offices sincerely and tirelessly in the Spirit of Christ" (para. 13). This teaching of Vatican II seems to move from monastic spirituality to one that flows out of our ministry. It suggests that this ministry of making people holy has the reciprocal effect of making the priest holy, of leading him to spiritual integrity and maturity.

In arguing in favour of a special spirituality for the diocesan priest, Robert M. Schwartz gives the example of Archbishop Romero of El Salvador. Born to privilege and remote from the suffering of his people, as a young bishop

Romero was profoundly affected by the murder of a close priest friend by government agents. This friend's crime was working to bring justice to the poor of his country. This experience moved Romero to enter into the plight of his people, most of whom lived on the edges of life. Despite his background of wealth and privilege, he came to share in their lives. Each Sunday he preached in his cathedral against the social injustices and human rights violations seen throughout El Salvador. This deepened entrance into his ministry – his reflections on the meaning of the gospel as applied to the lives of his people – made Romero challenge the government leaders of his day to acknowledge and address the disparities of wealth in El Salvador along with the marginalization of most of the people. As a result of his refusal to keep silent, he was assassinated – probably by the military – as he celebrated Mass. Romero became a saint and martyr who continues to inspire the people of his country. He found his God and his spiritual life. He became holy by entering into the life of and ministering to the community he served – and by conversing with God about all he saw and did.

What I am trying to describe here is not some kind of second-rate spirituality. Rather, it is based on doing what Jesus did, as described in Matthew's gospel:

> Then Jesus went about all the cities and villages, teaching in their synagogues, and proclaiming the good news of the kingdom, and curing every disease and every sickness. When he saw the crowds, he had compassion for them, because they were harassed and helpless, like

sheep without a shepherd. Then he said to his disciples, "The harvest is plentiful, but the labourers are few; therefore ask [pray] the Lord of the harvest to send out labourers into his harvest." (Matt. 9:35-38)

What is clear throughout the gospels, particularly Luke, is that Jesus retired regularly to pray, to converse with his Father. He presents a model of how his ministry of teaching and feeding (Mark 6:46, Matt. 14:23, John 6:15), of healing and choosing his apostles (Luke 6:12), is brought to his conversations with God, to his prayer. The great moment of his Transfiguration is preceded by prayer (Luke 9:28-29). His final agony in Gethsemane, as he prepares to fulfill his mission, is offered in his prayer. The priest, in his own way, brings his ministry, his experiences as a pastor, enlightened by the reading of scripture, to prayer as he searches for the words God would have him speak.

Clearly, time set apart for prayer remain an essential part of our spirituality. Believing that our work is our prayer and that we have no need of formal prayer is the so-called heresy of good works.

William Shannon is a diocesan priest from the diocese of Rochester, in the U.S. He is perhaps best known as an expert on Thomas Merton. Having acknowledged that a diocesan priest's spirituality flows from his ministry, Shannon cautions, "... in order to know that I am finding God in the external activities of life does require some quality time of silence and solitude on my part just to enable me to realize that this is what I am doing." We need time for our own prayer if for no other reason than to use this time to reflect on how much God loves us. We need to hear God tell us that he loves us, just as any lover needs to hear these words from the beloved. We also need this time to hear and see the grace of God that plays itself out in our lives and in our work. We must catch the signals of God in our lives.

The need for an interior life is obvious. Indeed, in these disjointed times of ours – these times of seeking and waiting, these days in the desert – it is not only Karl Rahner who suggests that the only Christians who will survive will be the mystics. Latin American theologian Leonardo Boff writes,

> Mysticism is not the privilege of the fortunate few. It is rather a dimension of human life to which *all of us* have access when we become conscious of a deep level of the self, when we try to study the other side of things, when we become aware of the inward richness of the other, and when we confront the grandeur, complexity and harmony of the universe. All of us, at a certain level, are mystics.

Our spirituality is *a spirituality of brothers*. In the secular and sometimes toxic culture that surrounds us, it takes great conviction to stand and pursue the way of the gospel. I doubt we will ever manage it if our spiritual life, this quest for holiness, is a flight of the alone to the Alone. Our spiritual life, like the hope that we preach, will always be a communal undertaking. It requires the support of our presbyterate and of the communities we serve.

Presbyterorum Ordinis says, "Established in the priestly order by ordination, all priests are united among themselves in an intimate sacramental brotherhood" (para. 8). To use a somewhat older language: whether we like it or not, through ordination we are ontologically joined at the hip! In *Pastores Dabo Vobis*, the document following the synod on priestly formation, John Paul II insisted that "The ordained ministry has a radical 'communitarian form' and can only be carried out as a collective work" (para. 17). Informing this spirituality that is uniquely ours as diocesan priests is the realization that we don't go it alone. Some sense of being with one another in one spiritual quest is needed. In a very real sense, when we pray, when we celebrate the Hours and the Eucharist, we do so not only with the universal Church but with our brothers in the local church. Even when we cannot be physically present to each other, on our best days we experience a sense of communal presence, of those close to us, of brothers who bounce off the walls of the places in which we pray.

If our charism is to make people holy, then we priests as brothers in the priesthood are first called to holiness together. In our common journey to holiness, we move ever closer to God, to one another and to creation. This is the wholeness for which we strive, the journey in which we are engaged. The spare language of the sometimes maligned Code of Canon Law, although it does not avoid the language of "perfection," enjoins us simply to "seek holiness" in our lives (Canon 276).

Our distinctive spirituality as diocesan priests flows out of a holiness resulting from serving the people of God. Fulfilling the privilege of this ministry each day leads us to be holy.

4

Solidarity, Obedience and the Church of the Diocese

In most of the world we inhabit, the concepts of solidarity and obedience do not usually win any standing ovations. As we swim in the waters of contemporary society, the danger is that we remain largely unaware of how insidious the culture of individualism is. As priests, most of us probably consider ourselves to be obedient and working together. We may hardly notice as we wander along that we are humming Frank Sinatra's "My Way" or following our own beat on our iPod.

Before we delve into this topic, let us examine these terms in some detail.

Obedience is not simply submitting to someone else's idea of what needs to be done. It is about aligning our will and desires with the will of one or more others.

The Letter to the Hebrews has much to say about priesthood, especially the priesthood of Jesus. He provides a
model of obedience that we can strive for. In chapter 10,
the author of this letter puts into the mouth of Jesus the
words of Psalm 40:

> "Sacrifices and offerings you have not desired,
> but a body you have prepared for me;
> in burnt offerings and sin offerings
> you have taken no pleasure.
> Then I said, 'See, God, I have come to do your will,
> O God.'" (Heb. 10:5-7)

We priests acknowledge that this finally is what
obedience is about: "I have come to do your will." At its
heart, obedience is the difficult and ongoing surrender
of our life to God. Like Jesus, we know that this action
is more important than sacrifice. Sometimes it seems like
the ultimate sacrifice!

As in much of life, there is always some ambiguity in
our obedience. We often wonder, "Am I being obedient
to the call of my life and of my God, as Jesus was? Or am
I simply obeying some of the powerful drives deep within
my unconscious? Am I being obedient to God, or to my
will to power, or to the will to give meaning to the ministry
I create?" Some of the ambiguity in obedience is reflected
in Jesus' story in Matthew's gospel when he spoke to the
scribes about the true nature of obedience to God.

> "A man had two sons; he went to the first and said, 'Son,
> go and work in the vineyard today.' He answered, 'I

will not'; but later he changed his mind and went. The father went to the second and said the same; and he answered, 'I go, sir'; but he did not go. Which of the two did the will of his father?" (21:28ff.)

We all have our ways of being obedient. There is probably something of both sons in all of us.

We know that obedience results from a call we have answered – a call that keeps sounding. We know that ours is a promise and a commitment for life. This very notion sounds strange in a society that seems to have a shelf life for almost everything and is almost neurotically averse to saying "forever." A priest's obedience, meanwhile, is submission of our lives forever.

In his book *Jesus of Nazareth*, Pope Benedict says that a dimension of loving God is what he calls "remaining." He goes on to say,

What the Church Fathers called *perseverentia* – patient steadfastness in communion with the Lord amid all the vicissitudes of life – is placed centre stage here. Initial enthusiasm is easy. Afterward though, it is time to stand firm, even along the monotonous desert paths that we are called upon to traverse in this life – with the patience it takes to tread evenly, a patience in which the romanticism of the initial awakening subsides, so that only the deep, pure Yes of faith remains. This is the way to produce good wine. After the brilliant illuminations of the initial moment of his conversion Augustine had a profound experience of this toilsome

patience, and that is how he learned to love the Lord
and to rejoice deeply at having found him."

This is what obedience is all about.

On the day of ordination; the new priest kneels before
the bishop and promises obedience. In recent years, this
vow of obedience in religious life and in the priesthood
has come under careful scrutiny. Some writers have dis-
missed this promise of the diocesan priest as a vestige of
a feudal society in which the vassal promised fealty to the
lord bishop. But this interpretation is overly simplistic.
There is more to our promise of obedience than a leftover
practice from history.

I would like to suggest that like many of the important
promises we make in life, the full import of the promise
of obedience at ordination becomes clearer as we live it
and pray about it and reflect on its meaning. Promises are
often made with only partial recognition of the cost and
meaning and everything the promise implies. Like celibacy, obedience is promised without full comprehension
of what it means. For many priests, I suspect that both of
these promises are accepted as part of the package.

Even in its strictest interpretation, obedience was
never meant to be blind – the slavish following of the
dictates of the bishop or religious superior in charge.
When discussing the obedience of the priest, a footnote
in *Presbyterorum Ordinis* underlines that our obedience is
not meant to mirror a child–parent relationship. It does
not, the document says, "... lead to infantilism nor make
him a cautious yes-man, but rather enables him to breathe

more fully the free air of the sons of God. It does not make him a puppet without initiative of his own" (para. 15, note 183).

One dimension of this obedience that has become clearer in recent years is that there is more to this promise than a pledge or a commitment made only to the bishop. It encompasses obedience and commitment to the Church, and especially to the Church understood as the people of the diocese within which the priest serves. It is also a promise and commitment to work together with, in solidarity with, brother priests. In promising obedience to the bishop, we promise to accomplish our shared charism of helping to make holy the people in our care, including ourselves. As we saw in the previous chapter, the Church is first and foremost as a community of people: the people of God. This understanding of the Church allows us to see obedience as seeking to set our own desires and our own will in line with the mission of the local Church and its people, in communion with all the presbyterate and under the leadership of the bishop. Our obedience, then, is offered with a sense of solidarity or unity with the people we serve, with our brother priests, and under the guidance of the bishop.

Solidarity is another key concept in Christianity, for Christianity is never a solitary exercise between an individual and God. We journey together, as a community, with our baptized brothers and sisters. With them we form a priestly, a prophetic and a kingly people witnessing to the activity of God among us. Further to this shared baptismal community, *Presbyterorum Ordinis* says, "Established in the priestly order ... all priests are united among themselves in an intimate sacramental brotherhood" (para. 8). As well as journeying together with all our baptized brothers and sisters, we are on a distinctive journey with our ordained brothers. In striving for some unity in purpose, attitude, opinion and interest, we express solidarity with each other under the leadership of the bishop. It is not so much I as an individual but we the presbyterate who, with the bishop, minister to God's people. As we have seen, our obedience is not only to the bishop but also to our brother priests and the people we minister to; that is how and why it is in solidarity that we are obedient to God.

A powerful sign of this solidarity is visible at the ordination of a new confrere, when each of us imposes hands upon the ordinand. This action acknowledges that what we are and what we do is shared now with this new brother. Whether old or young, ordained 50 years or 50 days, we strive to understand how each other thinks and feels and goes about ministry. We strive as often as circumstances allow to break bread and raise a toast with each other, knowing that brotherhood doesn't just happen. It is created by human gestures, few of which are more powerful than hospitality: eating and drinking together.

It is in solidarity as well that we accept and forgive one another's failings, acknowledging those brothers who have been sidelined for various reasons. We have always been tolerant and forgiving of confreres who have been known to toast a friend too often, who have strayed from their promise of celibacy, whose holiday schedule seems somewhat exaggerated, or who seek out the wealthy or seek wealth inordinately. When it comes to the sins of sexual abuse by clergy, we have perhaps shown less solidarity. Perhaps this is because our reputations and vocation have been besmirched by the conduct of a colleague. At times, we would appear to have left by the side of the road our confreres who are accused of sexual abuse. While we do not condone this destructive behaviour, we must ensure that those accused receive fair treatment and are not presumed guilty. As we offer care and compassion to the abused, we must not forget to offer the same to the accused, especially if he is convicted. No sin is unforgivable in God's eyes.

We also recognize the oneness of mission with priests, both diocesan and religious, who fulfill their ministry in tasks outside of parishes. The typical generosity that the latter exhibit in assisting their confreres in parishes is a sign of their sense of common mission with parish priests.

If we believe that we are one presbyterate, that we are in solidarity with all the priests of the local Church headed by the diocesan bishop, then we are, in fact, speaking of obedience to each other and to the people we serve, as well as to the bishop. Obviously, all this has much to do with our relationship to each other and to the bishop. Even more importantly, it depends on our theological understanding of the diocesan Church as a communion of people sharing in God's life; the diocesan Church as a sign and sacrament of the presence of Jesus; the diocesan

Church that *Christus Dominus* describes as "a particular Church in which the one, holy, catholic, and apostolic church of Christ is truly present and operative" (para. 11). This is the Church, the people of God, that the bishop together with his presbyterate is first called to serve.

Obedience understood within this context is about a group of priests, a bunch of men, doing something together, fulfilling a mission together. An old philosophical principle, *agitur sequitur esse*, speaks of acting in accord with the way we are, the way we understand ourselves. How we are diocesan Church and how we understand its mission will determine how we function in obedience to the people, to each other and under the leadership of the bishop. Embedded in this notion of solidarity in obedience (or obedience in solidarity) is that we have not just an implicit but an explicit common vision of the local Church and its mission and have jointly arrived at this vision. To make such solidarity possible, we must determine, agree on and commit ourselves to a common set of priorities. Within this mission, a priest's individual priorities and talents function in service of God's people.

To be obedient in a reasonable way, and to work in solidarity with brother priests, we must become well informed not only about our own parish, but about the nature, needs and consequent mission of the local and universal Church. Obedience and solidarity demand that the priest strives always to see beyond "his" parish, to avoid seeing it as an owner-operated franchise. We must be aware of the problems, the strengths and weaknesses not only of the people within our own parish, but of the diocesan Church and the universal Church themselves. To understand the shifting environments around us and the people we minister to, we must read the mail and e-mail from the diocese, go on the Internet, tune into the TV and radio, and peruse the newspapers, both secular and religious. We must be aware not only of the news, but of arts and culture, which feed people's spirits. In other words, we must make sure we have the periscope up rather than our heads in the sand. We must use whatever ways we can to know better the people we serve.

One approach is to make parish visits. Most priests don't do this anymore – there are too few priests for this time-consuming ministry. But my experience has been that few things reveal the needs and strengths of a parish more than visiting the homes of parishioners. When we spend time in their homes, we get a sense of the words of compassion and support people crave in our preaching. We touch close up the real environment in which the people who are the Church live much of their daily lives. Priests who get close to the families and single people in their diocese through home visits have a better sense of their pastoral priorities, which they can share with their brothers in the priesthood.

Here and elsewhere, all that we learn, we pray about. In this way, we grow increasingly attentive to the needs of the people we minister to and obedient to the Spirit of God working among us.

A cooperative, collegial, obedient approach to being a priest is not easy. Working in solidarity with one another is seldom a walk in the park. It is challenging not only in practice but even in theory. After four years of struggling with the question of episcopal collegiality – of bishops working together in solidarity – the Vatican II Fathers never really got the relationship of collegiality straight. The connection between their responsibility for their own dioceses and for the universal Church, together with each other and with the Holy Father, did not get worked out in any detail. This lack of clarity is reflected in the ongoing tensions around centralization and decentralization of decision making. For example, who makes decisions regarding pastoral practice and needs in dioceses around the world? The age at which children celebrate First Reconciliation, the use of general absolution, and the English translation of the Roman Missal are currently decided in Rome, not by local bishops or episcopal conferences, which have a valuable understanding of the local context.

The same kind of push/pull struggle can be found in our understanding of how the presbyterate, pastoral councils, and other collaborative structures at the diocesan and parish levels should function.

In the Western world, these relationships are further complicated by the fact that the Church does not fit easily into the democratic models that we have been taught to admire as the ultimate form of human governance, and that many feel must be exported to all parts of the world.

We still have a few miles to go in determining how we reconcile all that is good in the participation that democracy invites and in our Church as a hierarchical organization.

It helps to remember that the Church did not, like Athena, spring full blown from the mind of Zeus – or the promptings of the Holy Spirit! Beginning with the writings of the New Testament, it is clear that over the centuries, the role of Peter and his successors – and their relationship to the apostles and their successors – has been modified and clarified over time. The forms of Church government in the Acts of the Apostles are different from those of the Middle Ages, which are different still from ours today. Even Vatican II's document on the Church, *Lumen Gentium*, is incomplete and points to the future. This development of the Church's self-understanding and forms of governance is well documented in Richard McBrien's 2008 book, *The Church: The Evolution of Catholicism*. What form the Church and its parishes and dioceses will take remains a work in progress. The same can be said of the way we understand solidarity with one another, with our parishioners, with the people of the diocese, with the bishop, and with the Pope, and the way we honour our promise of obedience.

Let us take a closer look at the relationship the diocesan priest has with his bishop. Alexander Carter, a former bishop of Sault Ste-Marie, won the respect and admiration of the priests of his diocese and throughout Canada for the vision of Church and priesthood that inspired him. He was fond of saying that ultimately, the relationship of priests and bishop was always a love-hate relationship. What he seemed to mean was that priests know almost innately, without reflecting on the theology of the presbyterate, that they are intimately involved in and part of the bishop's ministry. They share in the same sacrament of orders, in the priesthood of the bishop. They serve the same local Church. They refer to him in every Eucharist at which they preside. Priests make the same type of commitment to the people as does the bishop. And because they are so much one with him, they have high expectations of him. When he exhibits the pastoral leadership of an apostle, we all succeed in our ministry; and we love him for this. When he seems to fail to live up to these high expectations we all fail. Interestingly, the survey data of Monsignor Rossetti referenced in Chapter 1 indicates that happiness in the life of a priest relates directly to satisfaction with his bishop and with Church leadership.

There seems to be some ambiguity in the Roman documents about the essential nature of this relationship between priest and bishop. The language used in *Priesthood: A Greater Love*, the 1995 document issued from the International Symposium of Priests and Bishops that commemorates the 30th anniversary of *Presbyterorum Ordinis*, seems to lean towards the authority of the bishop. It speaks of the bishop "as the authority figure of father and as friend." Thirty years earlier, *Lumen Gentium* suggested that priests "look upon the bishop as their father" and advised the bishop to "regard his priests ... as sons and friends" (para. 28). *Presbyterorum Ordinis* itself tells us that "the bishop should regard priests as brothers and friends" (para.

7). It is worth reflecting on the nature of this relationship. Should we regard the bishop as father? as brother? as friend? Clearly, it is difficult for any bishop to be at once the proper authority and father, friend and brother.

Obedience and solidarity are complex attitudes. Every priest knows that there are times when he must eschew the solidarity of brothers because he cannot agree with a decision or viewpoint. Likewise, obedience to the bishop or any religious superior cannot be in violation of our own conscience. The Franciscan Michael Crosby questions whether in some cases, the prophetic nature of the role of the priest or any Christian requires us not to submit. He cites St. Francis and St. Clare as examples. When the Roman authorities sought to regulate and unduly control their religious foundations, St. Clare "believed she was obeying, even as she refused to submit, because her obedience to the Holy Spirit required repeated insistence on the validity of her life choice."

Crosby delivers a strong, even stern, rebuke to all clergy – priests and bishops – and religious who, through uncritical submission, would avoid the suffering of conflict. He makes clear that that prophetic behaviour flows only from a mystical contemplation that focuses its attention on the absolute holiness of God. He further insists on genuine love and respect for all those who exercise institutional authority in the Church. For Crosby, prophets can speak the truth only if they do so in love.

This matter of obedience and solidarity in the presbyterate is more than a question for theoretical discussion.

Even with incomplete answers or knowledge, we are called to live in solidarity with one another and the bishop and our people and to obey God's call. The fact that we are a Church and a society in transition does not excuse us from grappling with these difficult questions.

Fulfilling our promise of obedience in solidarity with the people of the diocese, with the bishop and with each other surely is linked to that distinctive spirituality of the diocesan priest we examined in Chapter 3. If our spirituality arises out of our charism of helping people to become holy, then we will be obedient to this charism. With our bishop and brother priests we will seek to carry out our mission to serve all God's people. We will have a firmer grasp of these words of Jesus:

> "You know that among the Gentiles those whom they recognize as their rulers lord it over them, and their great ones are tyrants over them. But it is not so among you; but whoever wishes to become great among you must be your servant, and whoever wishes to be first among you must be slave of all." (Mark 10:42-44)

Within the freedom of the gospel, it is to this slavery that we are called through obedience and solidarity.

Charity and the Many Loves of the Priest

Up to this point, our reflections have centred on the priest as called to sanctify or make holy the people he serves. This ministry is accomplished in solidarity with the bishop and our brother priests in the diocese. It is essential, particularly in our present climate, that the priest be strengthened by and ever speak of hope. Our examination of the contemporary social and ecclesial environments makes obvious that this is a challenging task. Though important, such things as time for prayer, a thoughtful reading program, a Protestant work ethic, self-discipline and professional skills alone won't cut it when it comes to accomplishing our mission.

Ultimately, we must be men of many loves. We must love God, love the people we serve, love our friends, love our brothers in the priesthood, and love ourselves – as imperfect and as ambiguous and as tattered as this love may be at times. This love will reflect our personality. In some it will be more intellectual; in others, more emotional. In some it will flow from steely resolve; in others it will pour forth from an overflowing heart. Jon Hassler's novel *North of Hope* describes two priests, Adrian Lawrence and Frank Healy. They are both good men and good priests, but in very different ways. In an article in *America*, Andrew Greeley quotes Hassler himself, who comments on the two priests:

> One way to take the measure of goodness is to look at the way various people handle their vocations .... While the elderly Adrian Lawrence leads his life of loving kindness, impervious to doubts and difficulties, Frank Healy goes about his duties despite suffering through a dark night of the soul. "I've sprung a very big leak and my spirit is draining away."

Greeley says that given the strain Healy is under, "Frank Healy's service to others strikes me as the more heroic sort of goodness." Yet it is obvious that both Lawrence and Healy love the people to whom they minister.

For all of us, this love, this habit of the heart, this virtue of charity is a gift from God. It is hardly presumptuous to expect this gift to be offered to us in abundance given the ministry to which we have been called.

To love these many people, to have these many loves, we must first be convinced that we are loved by God, and then by those who are close to us: by good friends and family, the people we serve, and others we meet in life.

Henri Nouwen, one of the great spiritual writers of our time, talked often about "first love." He didn't mean that lovely creature I so longed for in Grade 11! Rather, Nouwen was convinced that the believer must first accept and experience God's prodigal and passionate and unconditional love before he or she can love as Jesus loves. Nouwen wrote this prayer:

> O Lord, look with favour on us, your people, and impart your love to us – not as an idea or a concept, but as a lived experience. We can only love each other because you have loved us first. Let us know that first love so that we can see all human love as a reflection of a greater love, a love without conditions and limitations."

There is really nothing new in Nouwen's prayer. His words reflect those of the First Letter of John: "We love because he first loved us" (4:19).

I think we were all impressed, edified and proud when Benedict XVI chose *Deus Caritas Est* as the title, theme and message of his first encyclical. He went to the heart of our Christian faith. The opening line of this encyclical also comes from 1 John, chapter 4: "God is love, and those who abide in love abide in God, and God abides in them" (4:16). When Benedict writes about this "first love" he uses unusual language. He speaks of God's passionate love for his people [which] ... is so great that it turns God against himself, his love against his justice. Here," the Pope says, "Christians can see a dim prefiguration of the mystery of the Cross: so great is God's love for man that by becoming man he follows him even into death, and so reconciles justice and love. (para. 10)

So this is first love – the love God has for us. We are loved long before our parents or siblings or teachers or friends or spouses loved us or hurt us. "I have called you by name ... you are mine," as the Grade 1 celebration in the *Come to the Father* catechetical program reminded the children.

Often, our experience of this first love comes through the warmth, security and trust of family. It happens in the intimacy of friendship, the passion of romantic love, or the companionship of confreres. Love touches us in the vast web of positive human relationships that make up the fabric of our life and our world. But in all these loves, and underlying them, is "first love": God's love for me.

We are capable of loving because we know that we are loved.

In speaking of who we are as human beings, we often quote the Book of Genesis, which tells us we are created in the image and likeness of God. Our scriptures and our theology define love as the essence of God. That is why it surprises us not at all that we are at our best when we love. At such moments, our lives reflect that we are indeed images of God. Instinctively, we know that we fulfill our humanity, are at once most human, most divine and most happy when we are in loving relationships.

The reason for this is simple: at these times, our true identity, our self, is revealed. In experiences of love, we touch the life of love shared by the Trinity – Father, Son and Holy Spirit – whom we have come to know through the human mind and heart of Jesus. In the moments we love, we are most like God.

Towards the end of *Deus Caritas Est*, Pope Benedict writes, "Love is possible, and we are able to practise it because we are created in the image of God. To experience love and in this way to cause the light of God to enter into the world ..." (para. 39). In our vocation of helping people discover holiness, we invite them to let God's light touch their lives. As we accompany them, we are witnesses to the epiphanies of God's love in their lives as infants are baptized, young lovers marry, seniors care for one another, and people reach out to others in so many ways.

Although we stumble often enough in our faith and in our personal journey, we know that we are loved. Love, or charity, is the mission and responsibility of the Church and, in a special way, our mission and responsibility. What does this mean for our own spiritual life and for our ministry? How does it affect the ways we love as we act as the Church's ministers?

Let's begin by talking about the love we have for the people to whom we minister. It's hard to get a handle on this love. In our homilies and sermons, most of us have probably commented on how our society uses the word love so glibly that it often loses all authentic meaning. When we speak of loving our parishioners, I think we mean that we have compassion for them. We share their many passions: their passion for life, their caring for spouse and family, their joy and celebration, their grief in times of sorrow.

We won't all do this in the same way. Some of us move naturally into the affective moments of those they serve. Others will remain more emotionally hesitant or detached. Yet we all can be with, be present to and stand beside our parishioners in the significant moments of their lives. That, finally, is compassion as all can practise it. The compassion of Jesus permeates the pages of the gospels. A prime example is found when he witnesses the agony and distress of the widow of Nain. Seeing the grief of this woman in the loss of her son, Luke's gospel tells us, "when the Lord saw her, he had compassion on her ..." – and he proceeded to raise her son back to life (Luke 7:11-17).

The charter and guidebook of our love or compassion is the Beatitudes. They call us to be compassionate with a pure heart, to be compassionate meekly, to be compassionate with a suffering heart, to be compassionate with the persecuted and the poor and the thirsting. Pope Benedict's book *Jesus of Nazareth* provides key insights into the meaning of such compassion, especially in the section on the Beatitudes.

Of course, we probably will never love everyone we serve with the same ease and commitment. The cantankerous old curmudgeon who complains about inadequate sand or salt on the church steps in winter doesn't elicit the same loving response as the attractive 25-year-old preparing for baptism. The obnoxious teenager knocking on the door and demanding bus money at 10:30 on a Saturday night does not summon the same loving response as the hard-working, ever-faithful president of the Catholic Women's League. Sometimes the compassionate response must come from a heart that is tired and dry and emotionally unresponsive to the person before us. That is when we know that loving compassion is a virtue or gift of God, a habit of the heart that we call charity. Like all habits, it deepens with practice.

I suspect that to love or act with compassion toward our parishioners requires us to be less hurried than the world usually demands. We must learn not only to listen but to pay attention to what people are saying. We must make time for them, and allow them space to tell their story. And we must recognize their saintliness. All these aspects are part of compassionate love.

A second love for priests is love for friends. I believe that compassion can be the abiding mark of our ministry only if we have friends — at least a few people with whom we can dare to be intimate. Usually, they are few in number. Only in Hollywood are 500 intimate friends invited to the party! Some friends may be men and some may be women. With certain friends we can be more intimate than with others. In most cases, one or more brother priests are intimate friends.

With our friends we share our vision and our deep feelings about what is important in our lives. We let down our defences and allow our vulnerability to surface, or at least to peek out. At least to some extent, we share our truth with friends. We may have moments of profound self-revelation in their company, but may tend to reveal our self and our soul in a light or humorous or even playful fashion rather than in anguished soul-searching. Having intimate friends allows us to touch the centres of love in our hearts and souls, so we can be compassionate pastors.

Even aside from how friendship helps us to be better pastors, the love of friends reveals the experience of a loving God in our lives. In his book *The Four Loves*, C.S. Lewis says that friendship "is the instrument by which God reveals to each the beauties of all the others. They are no greater than the beauties of a thousand other men; by Friendship God opens our eyes to them." In doing so, God opens our eyes to himself. Lewis describes true friends as companions on the journey. Rather than standing as lovers looking into each other's eyes, Lewis says that friends stand side by side, looking ahead together to where life is calling them.

In my experience, not many priests choose to stand apart from their brother priests. There are not many Lone Rangers among us. Perhaps in my diocese in northern Ontario, the geography makes us aware of how painful loneliness can be, and how community or solidarity is part of our vocation. We are thankful that priests are friends with one another and hospitable to each other.

Psychologists say that among friends, there is usually some level of sexual or erotic attraction, although we may not be conscious of it or may choose to ignore it. This remains as true for the priest as for anyone. We can fall in love with a dear friend. This leads us to a second promise we make at ordination: celibacy. As we live out our vocation, we do well to reflect on how we love as celibates.

This is not the place to discuss whether the Western Church's present discipline best serves the pastoral needs of the people we are called to serve. Or whether the current law, which requires all Roman Catholic priests to embrace celibacy, is an attempt to legislate a charism. Plenty of ink has been spilled on these questions. I will only tip my hand with this comment: at the 2008 World Eucharistic Congress in Quebec City, as we celebrated the Eucharist as the source and centre of Catholic life, some wondered how many Catholics in this country and elsewhere were deprived of this source and centre of Catholic life because of the shortage of ordained priests, which is at least partially caused by insistence on the law of celibacy.

For us ordained priests today, the promise of celibacy is a reality. Along with the promise of obedience, we may have embraced celibacy fully conscious of ourselves as gifted with this charism, or simply as part of the package of ordination to the priesthood. There is no doubt that celibacy is a gift to an individual and a gift to the Church that offers profound witness in a world caught up in the material and emotional gratification of the present moment. The modern mantra seems to be, "I want my new dining room set or new car or my double fudge chocolate sundae or sex – and I want it now!"

Many of us have found that our words as preachers and announcers of the gospel have lost their power to transform. Words are often not trusted – perhaps because in our time there has been too much perversion of the truth. Celibacy and obedience, however, are countercultural words. They ask questions that *are* heard in our world. The questions they raise break through the deafness of many, allowing the word of the gospel to seep through. Celibacy, in a society that wants everything, is a form of poverty. As Ron Rolheiser says, "to sleep alone is to be poor .... To sleep alone is to be outside the norm for human intimacy and to acutely feel the sting of that." Celibacy makes a statement that our world and our parishioners hear. I sometimes suspect that the venom that often accompanies attacks upon celibacy is triggered by a wish to put aside the questions raised by the committed celibate.

Some among us feel they have been blessed by God with this unique gift and charism of celibacy. Others have accepted it as a necessary condition of the call to the priesthood. For the latter, the path of celibacy is uphill and rocky. Yet all priests have moments of loneliness. There are days and even weeks that are bleak, when being alone with God doesn't answer our need for intimacy. Even for those with the charism there is many a lonely night, especially in the dark of winter as the snow flies and the temperature drops. This is true for the gay priest and for the straight priest. But for all of us, endowed with the charism or not, the call to love as a celibate remains.

Jonathan Sacks, the chief rabbi of Britain, has a marvellously simple saying: "We are here because someone wanted us to be here." As priests, we are here because God wants us to be here. That is the ground upon which we stand. Whether we are gay or straight. Whether we have kept our promise or broken it in one way or another. We stand upon God's holy ground as celibate ministers. And we stand on this ground; we are here, because God wants us to be here. So what are the consequences for living celibacy, whether or not we feel we have the charism?

One consequence is to accept that the path we follow is not natural. In *Deus Caritas Est*, Pope Benedict says, "… *eros* is somehow rooted in man's very nature; Adam is a seeker, who "abandons his mother and father" in order to find woman; only together do the two represent complete humanity and become 'one flesh'" (para. 11).

The celibate minister therefore acknowledges the innate power and mysterious beauty and goodness of sexual intimacy. He recognizes that the journey of sexual intimacy is the usual path to the human fulfillment we all naturally desire. He understands that for most people, this is the way of learning to love profoundly. So living celibacy in this sense is not natural. What the celibate does is take a leap of faith. He trusts that, according to the gospel, human fulfillment is often achieved by giving up the very things we naturally and legitimately desire. Using different words, and in various places in the gospels, Jesus' message to his followers reiterates the words of Matthew 10:39: "He who finds his life will lose it, and he who loses his life for my sake will find it." In seeking our ongoing growth and development as human persons, a second consequence of our celibate lifestyle is that we must trust these words.

A third consequence in the life of the celibate is temptation. There are the obvious temptations that result from the good and wonderful and powerful desire for sexual intimacy which itself is a gift of God. But there are other temptations, as well. One is to look upon human sexuality as something less worthy. There is, unfortunately, more than enough of this attitude in our Catholic tradition, but it is not the best of our tradition. Another is the temptation to maintain our promise of celibacy by keeping everyone at arm's length. Psychological profiles of priests indicate that many of us are naturally introverted. So it is tempting and, for some, easy to stand apart from others, especially women. Yet women powerfully incarnate the virtues preached by Jesus, particularly in the Beatitudes. Women, in my opinion, live a compassion that is attuned to human hurt. Without, I hope, offending feminist sensitivities, I believe that, whether by nature or nurture, women often seem less driven by the quest for power than men do, and women reflect the gentleness, meekness, poverty of spirit and compassion of the gospel. When we have good friends who are women, we experience the living of these gospel values, enrich our humanity, and enhance our practice of ministry.

Living celibacy as a commitment that estranges us and makes us remote from others can too easily lead to destructive forms of compensation. The denial of sexual intimacy leaves us open to excess in other creature comforts. We may be tempted to eat or drink to excess, leading to addiction or near addiction, obesity or other health problems. It is helpful to examine our lifestyle periodically, find healthy ways to cope with loneliness and stress, make a commitment to exercise, enjoy times of recreation, and so on.

Another consequence of celibate life is the need to be brutally honest with ourselves. We begin by acknowledging in our lives the power and wonder of human sexuality, in all its goodness and mystery. It helps to remember that sexuality is like dynamite: it can be used for good or harm. Our culture trivializes human sexuality, treating sexual activity in a casual way. Yet it is foolish not to acknowledge the raw power of sex and how profoundly sexual intimacy affects human life.

I don't share the opinion of some Freudians who suggest that human sexuality is everything, reducing all human activity and affectivity to our sexual drive. But it is true that as priests, even though we are celibate, we are sexual beings. We are loving, sexual persons. This means there must be something distinctive about loving as a celibate. And if there is something distinctive about loving as a celibate, it must relate significantly to our spiritual life, which in turn affects our ministry as parish priests. It is as celibates who love that we will fulfill our charism of making people holy. In the way we live and look upon celibacy, whether we feel we have the charism or not, whether we have been totally faithful to our promise or have wandered from it – wherever we find ourselves, there is work to be done. Whatever our personal situation is, it is as celibate pastors that we live out the ministry of helping people become holy. In our celibacy, as in the rest of our lives, we will ever speak the freeing word of God as wounded healers, as somewhat unfree men.

In all of this, what is not debatable is that we have to let other people into our lives if we are to be compassionate with our parishioners. We have to have friends – some of whom will become close friends – if we are to know the meaning of compassion and love. The possibility of an erotic attachment developing is real. The risk of failure in celibacy because of human weakness must be accepted – not sought after, mind you, but accepted! – as an almost inevitable part of our fallen human nature.

Seventeen centuries ago, one of the most celebrated Fathers of the Church, St. Ambrose, wrote in his *Treatise on Cain and Abel* that there is within each of us a "room where you hide your thoughts, where you keep your affections. This room of prayer is always with you, wherever you are, and it is always a secret room, where only God can see you." Henri Nouwen, Donald Cozzens and the Jesuit George Ashenbrenner all speak of a certain empty space in our hearts that only we and God can touch. It is an emptiness for God and it comes from the creator God. In talking about this space in the heart of the celibate priest, Cozzens shares these telling words: "The emptiness which celibacy creates in the heart of the priest can give birth to a cold and distant man, or the empty room inside can become a place of hospitality where God is welcomed and the people of the Church are gathered." Part of our prayer and reflections is always about our hospitality to God, to the people of our parish, and to our brother priests in that empty room within our celibate hearts.

I began by suggesting that our ministry will work only inasmuch as we love God, love the people we serve, love our friends, love our brothers in the priesthood, and love ourselves. These are the many loves of the priest. In our daily lives, we must seek to foster all the love we can manage.

Perhaps our prayer for one another could be the inspiring prayer in the Letter to the Colossians – a prayer of encouragement to all who follow in the way of Jesus that has particular application to those who minister to God's holy people:

> As God's chosen ones, holy and beloved, clothe yourselves with compassion, kindness, humility, meekness, and patience. Bear with one another and, if anyone has a complaint against another, forgive each other; just as the Lord has forgiven you, so you also must forgive. Above all, clothe yourselves with love, which binds everything together in perfect harmony. And let the peace of Christ rule in your hearts, to which indeed you were called in the one body. And be thankful. (3:12-15)

*O*ur Way into the Future

As we look ahead, it is clear that many questions will continue to confront both priests and lay people. The process of searching for the answers will probably be as important as the answers themselves in determining the future of the priesthood. The questions include the relationship between priest and laity, the role of the Church in society, the vocations crisis and the greying and burnout of clergy, the emerging role of women, the present and long-standing discipline of celibacy in the Western Church, priesthood as a permanent calling, the variety of pastoral practices from parish to parish and from diocese to diocese, and more. Here we will address a few of these questions and suggest some deliberately tentative answers.

Underlying many of the contemporary challenges is the fact that although Vatican II said much about the laity and the episcopate, its teachings on the priesthood were somewhat incomplete and ambiguous. The laity was acknowledged as "a chosen race, a royal priesthood, a consecrated nation, a people set apart" (cf. 1 Peter 2:4ff.). The role of the bishop was defined as being central to the understanding of ordained ministry. Further, bishops were seen as having a responsibility for the universal church together with the Pope.

In *What Are They Saying About the Ministerial Priesthood?* Daniel Donovan points out that, in the late 1960s, the prevailing opinion was that priests were, by and large, overlooked by Vatican II. He begs to differ, however. In his opinion, the council documents have much to say about the ordained or ministerial priesthood. This teaching, he points out, represents "a shift away from the theological model that has been dominant since the Council of Trent." This shift was symbolized in the revisions made to the very title of Vatican II's document on priests. As they pursued their discussion on the priesthood, the council Fathers moved from a document originally titled *De clericis* (On clerics) to one titled *De presbyterorum ministerio et vita* (On the ministry and life of priests). The emphasis was now on the priesthood as a service or ministry. Nonetheless, there continues to be concern that this council left much to be done in relation to its theology of the ordained or ministerial priesthood. In *The Church in the Making*, theologian Richard R. Gaillardetz examines some of the documents of

Vatican II 40 years later. He claims that "for all the council's many contributions, most of its energy on ordained ministry was spent on the episcopate, leaving little direction for a developed theology of the presbyterate ...."

Without entering this debate, I will highlight two major issues that address us with increasing insistence today: the way the priesthood of the faithful is understood in relation to the ordained priesthood, and the effects of declining numbers of clergy on the priest's day-to-day ministry and self-image.

The Ordained Priesthood and the Priesthood of the Faithful

In Chapter 2, we looked at how priests understand the question of the relationship of the priesthood of the faithful to what is variously called the ordained or ministerial or hierarchical priesthood. The Second Vatican Council gave renewed emphasis to the teaching that all the faithful share in the responsibility of teaching, guiding and sanctifying – that these roles are not restricted to the clergy. The council also insisted that by virtue of ordination, the priest was uniquely configured to the priesthood of Jesus Christ. In the words of *Lumen Gentium*, "They [priests] exercise their sacred function especially in the eucharistic worship or the celebration of the Mass by which *acting in the person of Christ* and proclaiming His Mystery they unite the prayers of the faithful with the sacrifice of their Head..." (para. 28). *Presbyterorum Ordinis* explains, "Wherefore the priesthood, while it presupposes the sacraments of Christian initiation, is conferred by that special sacrament; through it priests, by the anointing of the Holy Spirit are signed with a special character and are conformed to Christ the Priest in such a way that they can act in the person of Christ the Head" (para. 2).

The documents of Vatican II and subsequent Roman documents and theological development have insisted on two things.

First, there is a difference between the common priesthood or priesthood of the faithful and the ministerial priesthood. The latter involves a unique priestly configuration to Christ. As *Presbyterorum Ordinis* underlines,

> Inasmuch as it is connected with the Episcopal order, the priestly office shares in the authority by which Christ himself builds up, sanctifies, and rules His Body. Therefore while it indeed presupposes the sacraments of Christian initiation, the sacerdotal office of priests is conferred by that special sacrament through which priests, by the anointing of the Holy Spirit, are marked with a special character and so are so configured to Christ the Priest that they can act in the person of Christ the Head." (para. 2)

This is not to suggest that ordained priests are, by definition, holier than the people they minister to. They share the same call to holiness. But the ordained have an added responsibility: to serve the laity, particularly by helping all to follow this universal call to holiness. The priest ministers in order to sanctify or make holy the priestly community of God's people. The ministry of the priest, therefore, is not above but within the Christian community.

Second, Vatican II gave new prominence to the fact that the ordained are chosen from within this priestly community of the faithful. The call of the ordained is to serve this community and, in some cases, to act on its behalf. Priests are also called to act in the name of Christ and in the name of the Church. This they do by virtue of their ordination, which establishes them as sacramental ministers, especially as the ones who alone celebrate Eucharist. Not only is the priest a disciple, he also shares in the role of the bishop as apostle. As one who arises out of the community, the priest can experience certain tensions when he seeks to minister to and act on behalf of the community on the one hand, and act in the name of Christ or the Church on the other. In his service to the Christian community, the ordained minister, in other words, must also lead and guide and challenge it.

The laity we serve are highly educated, increasingly mature in their knowledge and their faith. They understand that, as God's people, they are not called to be passive objects, following someone else's direction. Rather, they are active subjects who will increasingly take on any number of missions and forms in the Church's life. Not surprisingly, tensions arise between priests and lay people from time to time. For example, a parish finance council may say that its financial responsibility extends only to administering and sustaining the goods of the parish. The pastor may challenge them to consider sharing parish monies with the diocese, the broader Church and society. Although parish councils and finance councils are determined by canon law to be consultative bodies, when lay experts with a democratic bent are told that the final word goes to the pastor, tempers can flare. We have a few miles to go as we try to dialogue, to foster a dialectic of co-responsibility and cooperation as the relationship between the laity and the ordained takes shape.

The Effects of Declining Numbers

As the number of priests continues to decline in Western society, the priest faces another contemporary tension: not enough time. People want the Eucharist and other sacraments. It seems that they want them before all else; not surprisingly, most bishops support this request. Catholics understand intuitively that the Eucharist is the source and centre of Catholic life. With fewer priests available, the priest's ministry – often not by conscious decision but through circumstances – becomes primarily a cultic one. He becomes a "Mass priest." Unfortunately, he does not have enough time for other dimensions of the priestly ministry, such as preparing homilies at a time when Catholics desperately seek a word that gives meaning to their daily struggles.

The disturbing bottom line when the ordained priest becomes identified almost exclusively with cultic functions is that this practice begins to shape his self-image, how he understands his own priesthood. He becomes a celebrant or a presider with little time to be a shepherd, guide and leader. The teaching, preaching and guiding functions are caught in the time squeeze. Only in sacramental functions does he have opportunity to break open the word of God; he is so busy with sacramental ministry, he has inadequate time to prepare for teaching and preaching. To make matters worse, all this occurs at a time when, as mentioned in Chapter 1, religious literacy, especially among younger Catholics, is low. And yet Catholics of all ages manifest a profound spiritual hunger. As the need for evangelization grows ever greater, the priest has time only for cultic functions.

This "Mass priest" syndrome affects everyone: priest and people. Even more importantly, it influences how Church authorities deal with the increasing shortage of ordained ministers in Western society. If the priest is considered primarily a cultic figure, then in times of clergy shortage, it is legitimate to diminish or reduce his ministry so that he functions almost exclusively as the sacramental presider or celebrant. His task is to ensure that the laity will have Eucharist on a regular basis and the other sacraments as needed. As he serves more and more people in this way alone, he becomes distanced from the underlying needs – the hurting, the longing, the wondering – and the festive moments of the people he serves. As a result, he doesn't know the people well, and he lacks the normal intimacy with parishioners that supports his own spiritual growth. If it becomes accepted that the primary role of the priest is to "say" Mass and confect the sacraments, then perspective is lost when it comes to the serious problems attached to importing priests from other cultures when homegrown priests are lacking.

If, however, the preaching and teaching roles of the priest are seen as being at least as important as his liturgical functions, our approach to increasing the number of priests must be more nuanced. Diocesan clergy are very grateful to priests who come from various parts of the world to serve the people in our parishes. Yet clergy who are new to the language and customs of the faithful may have more than linguistic problems when preaching and teaching. If they are unfamiliar with the local culture and idiom, it is very difficult to reflect on the gospel, to break open the Word and apply it to the life of the people. The 2008 Roman Synod had as its theme "The Word of God in the Life and Mission of the Church." In its final message, the synod insisted that the word must be clothed in the languages, concepts, symbols and religious traditions of the people to whom it is addressed (para. 15). Through no fault of their own, priests from other countries and cultures cannot easily accomplish this task.

This insight is not new. For years, missionaries from North America and Europe realized that they faced huge difficulties in ministering to people in foreign lands. A constant refrain of missionaries from Western countries was the need for an indigenous clergy who could minister, teach and preach in the language, culture and ways of their own people. These missionaries recognized that the people needed more than "Mass priests." It is unsettling, then, to witness Church leaders whose solution to the clergy shortage involves looking to places such as the Philippines, Africa and India to staff and serve our parishes. To my mind, this is but a stop-gap measure. There is a need to explore other initiatives to deal with this crucial issue in the Church.

There is yet another effect of clergy who are fewer in number and advanced in years. The majority of vocations to the priesthood result from young men being attracted to this life by the example of a priest or priests who are more or less of their generation. Such priests are familiar with youth culture, or at least with the interests and questions and searchings of younger people. Because of the lack of younger priests in many dioceses today, priests tend to be much older than the young people to whom they minister. It is more difficult for these priests to enter into youth culture, with its particular language, music, fashions and technological savvy. In his article "Religious Life in the Age of Facebook," Richard Molloy points out that a young person contemplating a vocation to religious life is faced with a situation in which "the average age in most communities has risen to a point where a young person is actually entering a retirement home, not a novitiate." Twenty- to 30-year-olds considering a vocation to the diocesan priesthood have few young priests with whom they can naturally relate. They would be joining a community of men, a presbyterate, whose average age is 60 or higher.

These same young people stand at an oblique remove from Church teaching on sexuality, human relationships and gender issues. The meaning of mandatory celibacy has not been part of their education, and indeed acts as a deterrent for young men who look forward to having a family. What they know of Church teaching on human sexuality they consider hopelessly out of date. They have been raised in a world where women are university presidents, accomplished professionals, heads of large corporations, and political leaders. Not surprisingly, they have difficulty with a Church that they see as marginalizing women.

Although it is wonderful to see the enthusiasm of young people as they partake in the much publicized World Youth Days, a quick glance around most parish churches on a Sunday reveals few of this generation. We seem to be in a Catch-22 situation: we need young priests who know youth culture to evangelize the young if we are to have new young priests.

I have written elsewhere that our young people today suffer from religious amnesia. Yet perhaps it is not so much amnesia – which implies forgetting something once known – as ignorance of the great stories and myths and the unconscious and imaginative habits of the heart of the Catholic believer. We are becoming increasingly aware that Catholics today – especially young Catholics – need to be evangelized, to hear the gospel message from the mouths and lives of believers.

First among these believers must be younger priests. There are many reasons why young people are distant from the Church. First and foremost is the fact that many of their parents are non-practising. Another is our secular culture, which encourages instant gratification and a tendency towards non-participation. However, a lack of younger clergy to whom youth can relate leaves bridges unbuilt between them and the Church. If for no other reason than the danger of losing more and more of our young people, our Church must find ways to attract more young men to the priesthood.

Faced with major problems that threaten the future of the priesthood – only two of which are briefly addressed above – priests and laity look to their bishops, our primary teachers in the faith. By listening with us to the signs and messages that our world and our Church are communicating to us, we can find solutions to these problems. Vatican II defined the nature and role of bishops: above all else, the bishop is a leader, guide and teacher. In today's Western society, this is not an easy task. Clergy and laity alike have much sympathy for the increasingly difficult task of their episcopal leaders. But we need them to teach us about the priesthood today. We need them to tell priests that bishops understand the increasing pressure under which priests labour, and to explain these problems to the laity. We need our bishops to encourage the lay members of the Church to accept their responsibility for providing candidates for the priesthood. Most importantly, from individual bishops and from regional and national conferences of bishops, priests need to hear their spiritual guidance and support in a public way: support for the huge majority of faithful priests who have had to bear the shame inflicted by a few of their number; guidance on the identity questions of priests whose ministry is reduced to a cultic one. Through pastoral letters and other public teaching, there can be raised an empathetic voice for the onerous burdens many priests carry as they tend to multiple parishes and other institutions.

To ask bishops to teach is a sign of respect for the episcopal office. We look to individual bishops and episcopal conferences to speak of the meaning and ministry of priesthood today – to speak of the teaching, preaching, guiding and cultic functions of the priest and how these relate to each other. While we sympathize with bishops who lack adequate numbers of priests, we want them to do more than what sometimes appears to be simply filling holes. Priests want something more. We want bishops who acknowledge and accept that they are indeed the successors of the apostles. Bishops who accept the responsibility of this historic office and exercise pastoral responsibility for their own diocese without looking over their shoulder. Bishops whose pastoral planning takes us beyond the status quo. Bishops who offer hope and encouragement and show courage. We want bishops who teach. As priests, we look to our bishops to lead and guide us in the task of making ourselves and God's people holy. We priests look for all this from our bishops whose ministry we share – a ministry that began with Jesus, was confided to the Twelve, and continues to this day.

Epilogue

The first chapter of this book began with a brief reflection on Christian trust: that God speaks to us always, particularly in the surround sound of life. In the signs that mark the passage of our journey, we hear the whisper of God's voice. It requires no great stretch of the imagination to suggest that one of those signs in our Church today is the drastic drop in the number of priests who minister, and the fact that those who do minister are, by and large, old men. Given this situation, is it too much to wonder whether God is not only speaking to us but taking us by the throat as he seeks to assure that the Church of the 21st century will truly be a Church of the laity? For us priests, this may be a difficult message. Yet, each day, we pray for the courage to be open to God's often challenging word. We begin our Office prayer daily with Psalm 95:

Today, listen to the voice of the Lord:
Do not grow stubborn,
as your fathers did in the wilderness,
when at Meribah and Massah
they challenged me and provoked me,
although they had seen all of my works.

In an article in *U.S. Catholic*, Richard Molloy SJ tells us that the average priest in the United States is 65 to 75 years old, and that by 2018, roughly half the priests presiding at Mass next Sunday will no longer be serving us. The situation is surely not much different in Canada and most Western nations. Molloy concludes, "How we imagine and prepare for a lay church now will greatly influence the survival of the church as community and institution beyond the 21st century."

In examining the ecclesial culture of our times in Chapter 1, we looked at how much the role of the laity in the Church had evolved in the 45 years since the close of the Second Vatican Council. It seems evident that intimately related to the development of the laity's role is the deepened understanding of the meaning and ministry of the priest. In Chapter 3, I suggested that the distinctive charism of the diocesan priest is assisting the laity in their quest for holiness: inviting them and helping them to undertake their priestly role of sharing in the teaching, guiding and sanctifying of their daily lives. It was to the laity that Vatican II particularly entrusted the Church's mission to "penetrate and perfect the temporal sphere with the spirit of the gospel."

The ministry of the priest in the 21st century will consist less in being in charge and more in discovering how best he can serve the people – all the people – who are the Church. At a time when belief is questioned and attacked both directly and indirectly, the ordained minister of the gospel will best serve parishioners by helping them to be comfortable within their own skins as believers and aware of their vocation to redeem the times in which they find themselves. In our secular age, the people who face the priest each Sunday morning are in many ways the *anawim*, the faithful remnant. They await the word of God. They are hungry for a word that is just, a word that rings out a message of human freedom and human dignity, a word that reflects the goodness of all that is beautiful and true in human life. This word stirs the Spirit of holiness that dwells within them.

The radical importance of preaching God's word will prevent the priest from being reduced to simply a "Mass priest." Presiding at Eucharist is central to the life of the Church. It is the priest's great privilege. Yet an essential dimension of that privilege is to distribute to the people we serve not only the Body and Blood of the Lord, but his Word as well. In doing so, we lead our parishioners and ourselves to holiness. As we define the role of the laity in the Church, the role of the priest emerges with a clarity that inspires that wounded healer, the priest, the servant of God's people.

$\mathcal{N}$otes

Chapter 1

I heard the Jack Kornfield story about the golf course in a talk given by Veronica O'Reilly CSJ to the religious men and women of the Diocese of London in 2007. Aileen O'Donoghue's comments from *The Sky Is Not a Ceiling* are found on pages 67–68. The quotation from Barack Obama's book *The Audacity of Hope* is found on page 39. Henri de Lubac is quoted in John W. O'Malley, *Vatican II: Did Anything Happen?* page 25. Richard Gwyn's words on knowing our history are taken from *John A: The Man Who Made Us*, pages 5–6. Monsignor Stephen Rossetti's words are found in "Becoming Priests for the First Time," *Origins*, July 3, 2008, page 125. Statistics from Andrew Greeley and other data in the paragraph are taken from Christopher Ruddy's work *Tested in Every Way*, pages 42–43. The reference to the foreword of Pope Benedict's book *Jesus of Nazareth* is to pages xi–xxiv. Sister Joan Chittister's phrase "we live in a desert between two places" is found in *The National Catholic Reporter*, December 31, 1999.

Chapter 2

Margaret Somerville's thoughts on hope are drawn from her article entitled "Dying: The Last Great Act of Living" (*The Calgary Herald*, March 9, 2009). Joan Chittister's words on hope are from *In Search of Belief*, page 149. Nicholas Lash writes of Abraham in *Seeing in the Dark*, page 11. Cynthia Bourgeault speaks of hope and tells the legend of St. Brendan in her book *Mystical Hope*, page 18. The sections of this chapter on prophesying, the temptation to make of God a magician, and the mystery of divine energy are paraphrased from an unpublished 2007 talk to the religious women and men of the diocese of London by Sister Veronica O'Reilly CSJ, the executive director of the Federation of Sisters of St. Joseph in Canada. James Carroll's words are taken from the *Boston Globe*, April 24, 2006. Joan Chittister's comments on Jesus' death are from *In Search of Belief*, page 136.

Chapter 3

John Paul II's words during a 2006 visit to Poland are quoted in Christopher Ruddy, *Tested in Every Way*, page 148. Joan Chittister's claim about spiritual arrogance is taken from *Welcome to the Wisdom of the World*, page 125. Parker Palmer's statement on wholeness is found in *A Hidden Wholeness*, page 5. Bishop Kenneth Untener is quoted in *The Spirituality of the Diocesan Priest*, Donald B. Cozzens (ed.), page 26. Daniel Donovan's writing on spirituality appears on page 16 of *What Are They Saying About the Ministerial Priesthood?* Ron Rolheiser's words are from *The Holy Longing*, pages 2–12. Richard McBrien writes in *Catholicism*, page 1057. Donald Cozzens quotes Abraham Heschel in *The Spirituality of the Diocesan Priest*, page 51. Writing in that same book, Robert M. Schwarz speaks of Archbishop Romero on pages 2 and 3. William Shannon is quoted in *The Spirituality of the Diocesan Priest*, page 94. Leonardo Boff writes in *Ecology and Liberation: A New Paradigm*, 1995, pages 147–48.

Chapter 4

The quotation from Pope Benedict's book *Jesus of Nazareth* is found on page 262. The quotation from the International Symposium of Priests and Bishops is found on page 20 of the document. Michael Crosby's words on St. Clare are from the last chapter of *Can Religious Life Be Prophetic?*

Chapter 5

Andrew Greeley comments on Jon Hassler's novel *North of Hope* in *America*, November 3, 2008. The quotation from Henri Nouwen is from *A Cry for Mercy: Prayers from Genesee*. C.S. Lewis's words on friendship are found in *The Four Loves*, page 105. Ron Rolheiser writes on sleeping alone in *The Holy Longing*, page 210. Donald Cozzens writes about celibacy in *The Spirituality of the Diocesan Priest*, page 19.

Chapter 6

Daniel Donovan's comments about priesthood are taken from page 3 of *What Are They Saying About the Ministerial Priesthood?* Richard R. Gaillardetz writes about Vatican documents in *The Church in the Making*, page 139. Richard Molloy's words are found in "Religious Life in the Age of Facebook," *America*, July 7-14, 2008, page 14. I write on religious amnesia among young people in *Catholic Education: A Light of Truth*, 2007, page 1 ff.

Epilogue

Richard Molloy's comments are from "The Word Made Digital," *U.S. Catholic*, December 2008, page 17.

Suggested Readings

Bourgeault, Cynthia, *Mystical Hope*, Cambridge, MA: Cowley Publications, 2001.

Catechism of the Catholic Church, Ottawa: Canadian Conference of Catholic Bishops, 1994.

Chittister, Joan, *In Search of Belief*, Liguori, MO: Liguori Publications, 1999.

————. *Welcome to the Wisdom of the World*, Ottawa: Novalis, 2007.

Cozzens, Donald B. (ed.), *The Spirituality of the Diocesan Priest*, Collegeville, MN: Liturgical Press, 1997.

Donovan, Daniel, *What Are They Saying About The Ministerial Priesthood?*, New York: Paulist, 1992.

Gaillardetz, Richard R., *The Church in the Making*, New York: Paulist, 2006.

Greeley, Andrew, *Priests: A Calling in Crisis*, Chicago: University of Chicago Press, 2004.

Lash, Nicholas, *Seeing in the Dark*, London: Darton, Longman and Todd, 2005.

Molloy, Richard, "Religious Life in the Age of Facebook," *America*, July 7-14, 2008.

Nolan, Albert, *Jesus Today: A Spirituality of Radical Freedom*, Maryknoll, NY: Orbis, 2008.

Obama, Barack, *The Audacity of Hope*, New York: Crown/Three Rivers, 2006.

O'Donoghue, Aileen, *The Sky Is Not a Ceiling*, Maryknoll, NY: Orbis, 2007.

O'Malley, John W., *Vatican II: Did Anything Happen?* New York: Continuum, 2008.

Palmer, Parker, *A Hidden Wholeness: The Journey Toward an Undivided Life*, San-Francisco: Jossey-Bass, 2004.

Pope John Paul II, *Pastores Dabo Vobis* (On the Formation of Priests), 1992.

Pope Benedict XVI, *Deus Caritas Est* (Encyclical letter on Christian Love), 2005.

————. *Spe Salvi* (Encyclical letter on Christian Hope), 2007.

Ratzinger, Joseph (Benedict XVI), *Jesus of Nazareth*, New York: Doubleday, 2007.

Rolheiser, Ronald, *The Holy Longing: The Search for a Christian Spirituality*, New York: Doubleday, 1999.

Rossetti, Stephen, "Becoming Priests for the First Time," *Origins*, July 3/08.

Second Vatican Council documents, especially:
- *Apostolicam Actuositatem* (On the Laity)
- *Christus Dominus* (The Bishops' Pastoral Office)
- *Gaudium et Spes* (The Church in the Modern World)
- *Lumen Gentium* (On the Church)
- *Presbyterorum Ordinis* (The Ministry and Life of Priests)

Taylor, Charles, *A Secular Age*, Cambridge, MA: Harvard University Press, 2007.